SPECTACULAR GOLF

WESTERN CANADA

THE MOST SCENIC AND CHALLENGING GOLF HOLES IN
BRITISH COLUMBIA AND ALBERTA

Published by

PANACHE
P A N A C H E   P A R T N E R S

Panache Partners Canada Inc.
1424 Gables Court
Plano, TX 75075
469.246.6060
Fax: 469.246.6062
www.panache.com

Publishers: Brian G. Carabet and John A. Shand

Printed in Canada

Distributed by Independent Publishers Group
800.888.4741

PUBLISHER'S DATA

Spectacular Golf Western Canada

Library of Congress Control Number: 2012930883

ISBN 13: 978-0-615-51926-5
ISBN 10: 0-615-51926-1

First Printing 2012

10 9 8 7 6 5 4 3 2 1

Right: Two Eagles Golf Course & Academy, page 41

Previous Page: Highland Pacific Golf Course, page 59

Panache Partners, LLC, is dedicated to the restoration and conservation of the
environment. Our books are manufactured with strict adherence to an environmental
management system in accordance with ISO 14001 standards, including the use
of paper from mills certified to derive their products from well-managed forests.
We are committed to continued investigation of alternative paper products and
environmentally responsible manufacturing processes to ensure the preservation of our
fragile planet.

SPECTACULAR GOLF
WESTERN CANADA

Sandpiper Golf Resort, page 91

FOREWORD

Canadians take both their homeland and their golf very seriously, and rightly so, given that there are few places in the world more extraordinarily beautiful and with as many challenges and pleasures as there are in Western Canada. Whether playing in Alberta on windswept prairie lands, on hillside courses of the majestic Rocky Mountains, or on the mountain and desert courses of the interior of British Columbia to the Pacific Ocean, golfers often find it difficult to keep focused on the game when some of the most remarkable scenery in the world is constantly competing for their attention.

Dating back to the colonization of Canada, when waves of early settlers from Britain, Scotland, Ireland, and the rest of Europe began to inhabit the land, golf became a sport of choice for many and was first played on Western Canadian soil in 1893. With the West's rich heritage and landscape, a number of the great golf architectural efforts crafted by some of the most recognized names from the Golden Age of course architecture—such as Stanley Thompson, A. Vernon Macan, and Robert Trent Jones Sr.—have left their signature designs, making this region one of those unique places that amalgamated spectacular land with our spirited game.

Born and raised in British Columbia, I never fully appreciated my devotion to Canada until, in spite of the travel challenges of playing the PGA Tour, my wife Joanie and I made the decision to move back to the province and raise our three children here, calling Vancouver home. The more I traveled the world as a tour professional, the more I came to appreciate just how beautiful and special Western Canada is.

Diversity is one of the many characteristics that makes this land so distinctive, which is an opinion I share with many other top-ranked professional and amateur golfers who have had the opportunity to play in this part of the world. From a global perspective, very few destinations can match the majesty of the courses near Banff, for example, where the experience includes incredible golf surrounded by spectacular natural vistas and wildlife. The diversity is nearly endless; where else can you ski at an Olympic venue then play 18 holes of golf in the same day?

Whether you experience golf in Western Canada's many genuine mountain terrains, play by the natural rivers and streams, or touch the soul of the rich ranching history, you will feel right at home. You will no doubt find this beautiful book an inspiration, as it captures all that is wonderful about our game. May *Spectacular Golf Western Canada* inspire you to visit and play these great golf courses.

Enjoy your game,

R. Zokol

Richard Zokol

Two-time PGA Tour winner, 2011 Canadian Golf Hall of Fame inductee, and co-designer/developer of The Club at Sagebrush

Quilchena Golf and Country Club, page 71

INTRODUCTION

The massive provinces of British Columbia and Alberta encompass some of the most diverse and photogenic topography not only in Canada but in the entire world. From the Pacific Ocean-splashed West Coast of Vancouver Island to the edge of the vast prairies in eastern Alberta, the terrain traverses saltwater marshes and freshwater meadows, rainforests and parklands, and rugged peaks and rolling hills, not to mention deep canyons and shallow arroyos, lush greenbelts and true deserts, table-flat plains and the soaring Rocky Mountains. Home to cacti and towering Douglas firs, rattlesnakes and grizzly bears, wheat fields and vineyards, British Columbia and Alberta have long been an irresistible lure to photographers, painters, adventurers, dreamers, and golfers alike.

For well over a century, the region's dramatic beauty has provided an incomparable canvas for the most artistic and celebrated golf course designers. *Spectacular Golf Western Canada* is a passport to a compelling journey through some of the premier golf destinations in the world. This collection of brilliantly designed and exquisitely photographed golf holes is eloquent testimony to why thousands of golfers from around the globe come to BC and Alberta each year to experience the magnificence for themselves.

And it's not just recreational golfers who are drawn to the area. Over the years, some of the finest players in the game have competed here, from Ben Hogan, Byron Nelson, Greg Norman, and Fred Couples to Jack Nicklaus—who has also designed exceptional courses here, including Nicklaus North in Whistler, BC—and current-era superstars like Phil Mickelson, Sergio Garcia, and Rickie Fowler. The PGA Tour's RBC Canadian Open has been contested three times at Vancouver's Shaughnessy Golf and Country Club, and the Canadian Professional Golf Tour, the Nationwide Tour, and LPGA's Canadian Open make regular stops in these provinces as well.

Inside are holes familiar not only to locals but also to international audiences that have enjoyed the men's and women's opens, Air Canada championships, and the popular Skins Games. Some lesser-known but just as outstanding gems are also waiting for you to discover within these pages.

The magnificent golf courses featured in *Spectacular Golf Western Canada* have been created by a veritable who's who of the game's finest designers like Jack Nicklaus, Robert Trent Jones, Doug Carrick, Thomas McBroom, A.V. Macan, Rod Whitman, Richard Zokol, Wayne Carleton, Graham Cooke, Gary Browning, Norman Woods, Les Furber, Bill Newis, and Canadian golf legend Stan Leonard. Without question, from the Pacific to the prairies, from the US border to the Rockies, "super-natural" BC and Alberta's Wild Rose Country, as the provinces are known to locals, are incredible regions for spectacular golf.

CONTENTS

Greywolf Golf Course, page 111

Sandpiper Golf Resort, page 123

BRITISH COLUMBIA

Nk'Mip Canyon Desert Golf Course, page 23

BRITISH COLUMBIA GOLF

604.279.2580
www.britishcolumbiagolf.org

Canada's westernmost province has a long and storied history in the game of golf that dates back to the opening of the first course in British Columbia at Vancouver's Jericho Beach in 1892. Just a year later, the BC Golf Association, now known as British Columbia Golf, was formed with the mandate to hold a provincial championship. In 1894, BC's first amateur golfing championship was held at the Victoria Golf Club. The winner was awarded a trophy donated by Hewitt Bostock, the lieutenant governor of the province. The trophy, known as the Bostock Cup, is still awarded today and is believed to be the oldest continuously competed for trophy in North America.

The first women's amateur championship was held in 1895, and 10 years later the champion was awarded the Flumerfelt Cup, which continues to be raised high overhead by each BC amateur women's champion. This trophy also boasts the title of North America's oldest continuously competed for women's trophy.

That proud legacy continues with more than 300 golf courses gracing BC's incomparable terrain. Some, like the venerable Shaughnessy Golf and Country Club, have celebrated their centennials while others, like the spectacular Wildstone Golf Course on the edge of the BC Rockies, are just starting to make history of their own.

In this remarkable chapter, some of the most beautiful and challenging golf holes in the world—designed by some of the game's finest architects including Jack Nicklaus, Doug Carrick, A.V. Macan, and others—unfold in their colourful splendour in one of the most historic and scenic golf destinations in the world.

Photographs courtesy of British Columbia Golf

St. Eugene Golf Resort and Casino, page 37

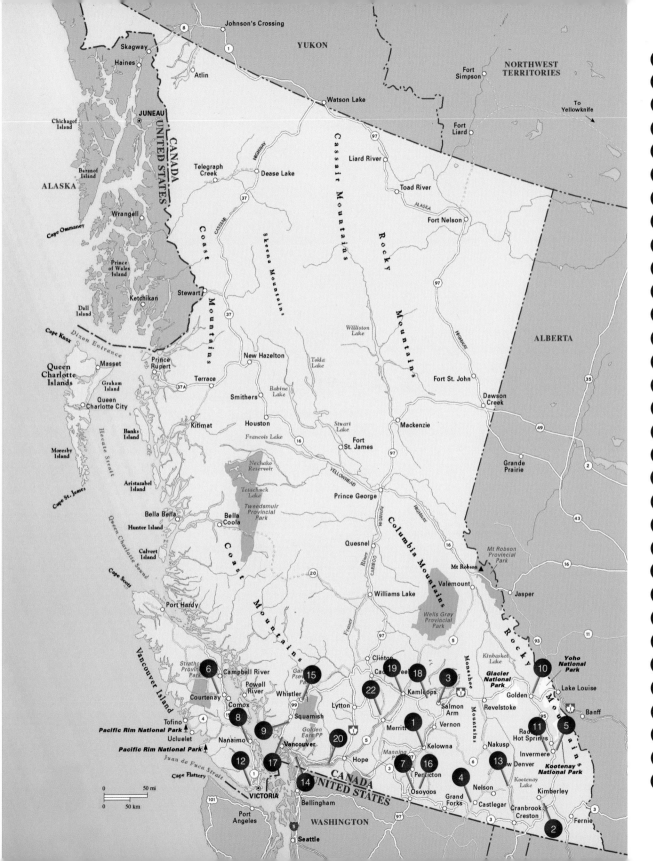

1 Black Mountain Golf Club
2 Bootleg Gap Golf
3 Canoe Creek Golf Course
4 Castlegar Golf Club
22 The Club at Sagebrush
5 Copper Point Golf Club
2 Cranbrook Golf Club
6 Crown Isle Resort & Golf Community
7 Fairview Mountain Golf Club
8 Fairwinds Golf Club
9 Furry Creek Golf & Country Club
1 Gallagher's Canyon Golf & Country Club
10 Golden Golf Club
11 Greywolf Golf Course
12 Highland Pacific Golf Course
13 Kokanee Springs Resort Club
14 Morgan Creek Golf Course
15 Nicklaus North Golf Course
16 Nk'Mip Canyon Desert Golf Course
17 Northlands Golf Course
17 Quilchena Golf and Country Club
20 The Redwoods Golf Course
19 Rivershore Estates & Golf Links
3 Salmon Arm Golf Club
20 Sandpiper Golf Resort
17 Shaughnessy Golf and Country Club
3 Shuswap Lake Estates Golf & Country Club
2 St. Eugene Golf Resort and Casino
18 Talking Rock Golf Course & Quaaout Lodge
1 The Harvest Golf Club
1 Two Eagles Golf Course & Academy
2 Wildstone Golf Course

BLACK MOUNTAIN
Golf Club

18 HOLE

PAR 5 ◆ 501 YARDS

Kelowna, BC
250.765.6890
www.blackmountaingolf.ca

The finale at Black Mountain Golf Club in Kelowna is known as the "grip it and rip it" hole. Architect Wayne Carleton tops off the club's theme of fun golf with the welcoming par-5 18th that leaves most players smiling. Most of the trouble is along the left side, so tee shots down the right side on this hole that measures from 501 yards down to 429 yards set up a chance to reach the green in two.

But they don't give away birdies or eagles, even at Black Mountain. Carleton had some fun placing 11 bunkers on 18; the three down the left, four on the right, and four guarding the green bring the course total to 66. A deep gulley runs along the entire left side of the hole. Shots into the gulley call for a reload.

Laying up and hitting a short iron into the green is always a wise option. The bunkers at the green are well-placed, with pot bunkers on either side and larger traps at the front right and back left. One of the biggest greens on the course, it is slightly elevated, two-tiered, and slopes away in the back left. The 18th is a fitting end to a fun round.

Photograph by Colin Jewall

CASTLEGAR
Golf Club

HOLE

PAR 5 ◆ 512 YARDS

Castlegar, BC
250.365.5006
www.golfcastlegar.com

With views from the plateau of the surrounding peaks and the Columbia River below, it is not surprising that the residents of the picturesque Kootenay Rockies city of Castlegar chose this site to build themselves a golf course. Since Castlegar Golf Club's first nine holes opened in the early 1960s, the now 6,712-yard 18-hole layout has matured into one of the province's most beautiful courses. With a rating of 71.8 and slope of 125, Castlegar is welcoming to all players and has tested the best by hosting the BC Seniors and BC Amateur Championships.

Because each hole was designed by a group of club members, the course is full of unique charms and challenges, offering wonderful variety. The par-5 second hole is typical of Castlegar: immaculately conditioned, possessing a character all its own.

From the downhill second hole's four tee boxes, which stretch it from 452 yards to a robust 512 yards, Red Mountain and the Rockies are in full view.

Long ball hitters have to worry about two waste bunkers that guard the right side of the fairway. The green slopes from the back to the front and is well protected by a tree on the left and a difficult bunker on the right. Second or third shots that go past the green leave a tough downhill chip. Be wary of pin placements in the right front portion of the green where putts can be very quick. Most players are very pleased with a par here, Casltegar's number one handicap hole.

Photographs by Don Weixl

GALLAGHER'S CANYON
Golf & Country Club

PAR 5 ◆ 524 YARDS

Kelowna, BC
250.861.4240
www.golfbc.com/courses/gallaghers_canyon

Gallagher's Canyon Golf & Country Club's layout, a classic mountain course designed by Bill Robinson, delivers the true Okanagan golf experience. Mature stands of ponderosa pine, undulating terrain, and the rugged background views for which the area is famous provide the setting for a memorable game each time out.

The 524-yard sixth hole encapsulates so much of what there is to like about Gallagher's Canyon. The green on this long par 5 ends on the verge of the canyon itself, offering a stunning vista with views of Mission Creek, the city nearby, and orchards laid out on the surrounding hillsides.

Number six is a classic risk/reward hole. The green is reachable in two, but the margin for error is limited. Fairway bunkers are situated on the left at the midpoint of the fairway. Approximately 90 yards before the green, a berm of deep fescue encroaches from the left to constrict the fairway and threatens to absorb the ball,

leaving players with a challenging lie for their approach shot. On the right side of the fairway, just opposite the berm, is another fairway bunker, so placing tee and second shots is critical to staying out of trouble. Trees flank the fairway on both sides, and to the left is out of bounds.

Perched on the edge of the canyon, the green is surrounded by bunkers and features an elevated bank rounded up off the rear edge in front of the canyon lip. Overshoot the green, and this is one time that hitting the bunker rates as a positive outcome, given what lies just beyond it.

Photograph by John Henebry

NK'MIP CANYON
Desert Golf Course

PAR 5 ◆ 602 YARDS

Oliver, BC
250.498.2880
www.nkmipcanyon.com

The natural beauty and dramatic landscapes of the northern tip of the Sonoran Desert are on full display from the tee boxes of the 15th hole at Nk'Mip Canyon Desert Golf Course. The massive McIntyre Bluff dominates the horizon, the Okanagan Range of the Cascade Mountains forms a silhouette in the distance, and the countless varieties of indigenous flora—including cacti, sage, "greasewood" pines, golden aster, and antelope brush—trace both sides of the lush green fairway.

Named "The chief" for its commanding presence, and the outline of an Indian chief's face and headdress on the upper right edge of the bluff, the 15th is a classic three-shot par 5 from the elevated black tees (602 yards), the blues (562 yards), the whites (518 yards), and the reds (492 yards). The landing area is generous, but the fairway gradually narrows as it rises gently toward the green.

There are no bunkers on this robust par 5. The natural vegetation, gentle slope, and arresting views are enough to earn the 15th the rank of second-most difficult hole on the canyon and grove nines that make up the fine golf course.

Nk'Mip is owned, built, and operated by the Osoyoos Indian Band. Wines from the Band's Nk'Mip Cellars—the only wholly owned Native Indian winery in North America—are proudly served in the beautiful clubhouse. A fine vintage from the cellars is a fitting reward for par, or better, at The Chief.

Photograph by Steve Austin

NORTHLANDS
Golf Course

4 HOLE

PAR 5 ◆ 531 YARDS

North Vancouver, BC
604.924.2950
www.golfnorthlands.com

As much as any of the holes at Northlands Golf Course, the fourth demonstrates Les Furber's accomplishments in retaining the natural attributes of the site and using them to enrich the golfing experience. The green is a favourite grazing area for deer, so have a camera handy.

The fourth is a 531-yard uphill par 5, possessing the greatest handicap on the entire course. A solid tee shot is very important. Few players have the distance required to hit the green in two, so plan on three solid shots to get there. On your second shot, aim for the waterfall for a great angle to the green. The refreshing mist drifting off the signature waterfall is an added bonus on warm summer days.

Take note of the pin placement on the narrow oblong green, which is well bunkered and 45 yards from front to back. The green's three-level organization makes club selection the key to scoring well. Any shot landing above the hole will create a great deal of tentativeness because you can easily be looking at a long return putt—the greens are fast and true. A side hill putt is always tricky and on the mountainous course's fourth hole you can expect severe breaks. Keep it below the hole and on the correct tier for a chance at par. Consider yourself a pro if you birdie this monster.

Photograph by Pablo Su

QUILCHENA
Golf and Country Club

PAR 5 ◆ 505 YARDS

Richmond, BC
604.277.1101
www.qgolfclub.ca

Quilchena Golf and Country Club takes its name from a First Nations word meaning "running water," "sweet water," or "many waters." Located snugly on the south arm of the Fraser River estuary, the course experiences a links-style wind challenge on many rounds. In keeping with the name, water plays a prominent role on this challenging par-5 hole with a pond guarding the right front and side of the green.

The second par 5 on the front nine, this hole is a dogleg left with tall, mature trees lining both sides. A fairway bunker on the right guides players around the corner, but a sober appraisal of the golfer's hitting power is very necessary. Only the longest hitters will have a chance to carry the water hazard and reach the green in two.

The spectacular hole offers great risk/reward, but a lay up in front of the water guarding the approach to the green is a good, safe strategy. Deliberate placement of tee and second shots takes precedence over raw power for most players, assuring a more predictable play.

Whether golfers are looking for a few casual holes in the evening, a championship round, or to play with a regular foursome for a few bucks, this course delivers all that could be desired—and then some.

Photographs © hux.net

RIVERSHORE ESTATES
and Golf Links

PAR 5 ◆ 537 YARDS

Kamloops, BC
250.573.4211
www.rivershoregolflinks.com

On the north shore of the South Thompson River, in the picturesque Thompson-Okanagan region near Kamloops, the legendary Robert Trent Jones created what is generally considered his finest links-style golf course. On broad, rolling bench land at the base of a range of rocky hills, Rivershore Estates and Golf Links lies amid the sagebrush and remnants of oxbow lakes. Since opening in 1981, the course has won awards, hosted numerous amateur and professional championships, and earned the acclaim of golfers from around the world.

The signature Jones design elements—long rectangular tee boxes, large bunkers, and big greens—are prevalent throughout Rivershore, with its 95 bunkers and water in play on five holes. The first hole to feature water is the eighth, a fairly short par 5 of 537 yards. The hole runs arrow-straight with out of bounds all along the left side.

A large bunker complex protects that side of the landing area, while trees, fescue, sage, and other indigenous flora border the right side of the fairway.

An old oxbow lake guards both the lay-up area and most of the front of the green that is very wide but extremely shallow and sloped aggressively from back to front. The middle of the green is set lower than the left and right sides rather like an inverted saddle. Bunkers guard those portions of the green not already protected by water. The eighth is a classic par 5 on one of Jones' finest courses.

Photograph © hux.net

SALMON ARM
Golf Club

18 HOLE

PAR 5 ◆ 504 YARDS

Salmon Arm, BC
250.832.3667
www.salmonarmgolf.com

At a little over 500 yards, the 18th offers a classic risk/reward scenario as a finishing hole that can make or break your game and alter the outcome of a friendly wager. Treed on both sides, this Les Furber-designed hole drops in elevation from tee to green. With additional mounding on the right and a 100-yard waste area on the left, you're challenged to make a solid tee shot.

Longer hitters will revel in the butterfly sensation in their stomachs as they set themselves up for a long second shot over water and a bunker fronting the wide but shallow green. The downhill lie heightens the importance of making clean contact. For golfers choosing discretion over valour, lay-up shots are hit to a narrow landing area where the short final approach shot over the pond must be struck confidently to avoid a watery grave.

A birdie or par will bring a smile to your face as you look down the fairway and savour your accomplishment. The clubhouse, a stunning backdrop as you leave the 18th hole, is your next destination to recount the ones you missed and the ones that made your experience so grand.

Photograph © hux.net

SANDPIPER

Golf Resort

PAR 5 ◆ 486 YARDS

Harrison Mills, BC
877.796.1001
www.sandpiperresort.ca

"Water" is the watchword on Sandpiper Golf Resort's signature number 15, a challenging, 486-yard par 5. Shot-making ability is definitely an asset on the hole.

Players must cross no fewer than three natural hazards that bisect the fairway between tee and green. Added to the streams are two sizeable ponds, one lurking just past the green on the right with a second running along the left side of the fairway.

A number of bunkers flank the fairway, most notably the footprint of the legendary Sasquatch also know as Bigfoot, purportedly an ape-like creature that inhabits the forests of the Pacific Northwest. This bunker that guards the approach to the green is larger than the green itself and leaves little margin for error. Footprint bunker left,

pond right, and stream crossing in front—controlled placement of the approach shot is essential. A confined safe landing area to the right front of the green is one possibility.

Mountains and river valley conspire here to make the wind a constant factor. A successful result is cause for satisfaction, if not uninhibited celebration.

Photographs by Doug Johnson

SHUSWAP LAKE ESTATES
Golf & Country Club

5 HOLE

PAR 5 ◆ 495 YARDS

Blind Bay, BC
250.675.2315
www.shuswaplakeestates.com

Capitalizing on the location's natural assets, Shuswap Lake Estates Golf & Country Club stands as a stellar example of a residential estates course. Family-run by its original owners since 1977, the scenic course weaves around elegant residential developments and an airstrip.

Recently expanded to 6,467 yards, the 18-hole course has much to offer: strategically placed bunkers, challenging greens, and four beautiful lakes making an impact on the play of almost half the holes.

Hole number 5 calls for both power and finesse. The elevation on this straight fairway rises from the tee and falls again toward the green. The hole is narrowly constricted near the midpoint by the trees that hug the fairway, lining both sides. Get past the constriction and the real test begins.

The green on number 5 allows no margin for error. Water guards the front of the green with little or no landing area between it and the edge of the green. Tight on the left rear side, a bunker awaits any shots that go long. Err to the right and the edge of the green falls off sharply into a deep treed hollow. This is one approach shot you definitely want to get right.

Of course, what makes the hole tough also makes it beautiful and a lot of fun to play. Don't forget to take a moment to relax, breathe in the fresh mountain air, and enjoy the valley and mountain vistas.

Photograph by Wendy Barker

ST. EUGENE 18 HOLE
Golf Resort and Casino

PAR 5 ◆ 558 YARDS

Cranbrook, BC
877.417.3133
www.steugene.ca

St. Eugene Golf Resort and Casino takes full advantage of its spectacular Rocky Mountain setting, where majestic pine forests and the St. Mary's River—a world-renowned fly fishing destination—provide a fitting backdrop for the championship layout. At a total yardage of 7,007 from the back tees, the par-72, Furber-designed course offers a rich variety of environments.

The 558-yard 18th hole's broad, straight fairway is ringed by hazards. A large area of rough bracken to both sides awaits any miscue off the tee. Across the front of the fairway and running the entire right side is a series of bunkers that make it critical to keep your ball within the fairway area. On the left, a prominent water hazard runs the length of the fairway. And while the fairway is broad and relatively flat, a substantial bunker lurks dead centre, forcing players to make a critical decision in selecting their strategy off the tee. A rough gulley crosses the front of an undulating green with bunkers on both sides. Hole 18 truly captures the spirit of the St. Eugene course: straightforward, but genuinely challenging.

Visually, the hole offers a stunning prospect. The resort's imposing architecture set against the towering snow-capped mountain is breathtaking. For what transpires during play as well as the experience of the course as a place to be, St. Eugene is sure to be memorable each and every time.

Photograph by Don Weixl

TALKING ROCK

Golf Course & Quaaout Lodge

PAR 5 ◆ 562 YARDS

Chase, BC
800.663.4303
www.quaaoutlodge.com

On the shores of Little Shuswap Lake lies the pride of the enterprising Little Shuswap Indian Band: Talking Rock Golf Course & Quaaout Lodge. The course opened in 2007 on the site known by the First Nations as "Land of the Great Spirit."

Course architects Graham Cooke and Wayne Carleton welcomed the task of developing a design that honours heritage and reflects natural abundance. The result: a 7,129-yard, par-72 course that's both challenging and accessible. Well-spaced fairways make the most of topography and natural growth.

Traditions of the past are represented, with Aboriginal art placed throughout the course. Sightlines from the elevated tee box on Talking Rock's signature seventh give little warning that there is a bear lurking in the fairway bunker—the outline of a grizzly bear in the centre of the sand trap, to serve as a spiritual reminder.

Three large fairway bunkers line the right side, making it a hole where you can grip it and rip it from the elevated tee box. Place your second shot in the middle of the fairway: anything left and the pine trees will block your approach to the oval green; anything right and you're looking at a complex third shot—over two right-hand bunkers. Prevailing winds off Little Shuswap Lake have captured many a ball and mean at least a club difference. Watch your approach. A ridge running through the middle of this small green makes the downhill portion quicker than it looks.

Photograph © hux.net

TWO EAGLES

Golf Course & Academy

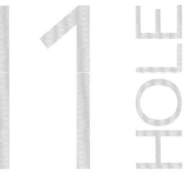

PAR 5 ◆ 528 YARDS

Westbank, BC
250.768.0080
www.twoeaglesgolf.com

Combining the championship qualities of a classic Les Furber design with the playability of a mid-length facility, Two Eagles Golf Course & Academy embodies a refreshing concept. Regardless of your age or ability, Two Eagles is an extremely friendly environment in which to learn, to grow, and to enjoy the game of golf.

Add in the rolling hills and ponderosa pines overlooking Okanagan Lake, and it is an experience you will want to repeat over and over. The style is reminiscent of definitive Les Furber designs such as Predator Ridge, Silvertip, and Trickle Creek, which use the natural landscapes to shape the golf holes. Typical of his courses, Two Eagles is strikingly visual in nature. "People best appreciate what they see," Furber says, "not what they know or think they know."

As you negotiate the two creeks, six ponds, 72 sand traps, and undulating bent-grass greens, you will find that no two holes present the same challenge. On the tee box of the 528-yard 11th, you're faced with a narrow gap featuring a soft dogleg left that is framed by majestic pines, a rocky creek meandering along the left side of the fairway, and a large bunker protecting the right side. A decision is now required on the tee shot: an aggressive line to take advantage of the par 5 or a conservative tee ball to lead to a third shot approach. Bunkers are well placed and capture many a ball for those attempting to hit the green in two shots. The three-tiered green makes accuracy and distance control very important for any birdie opportunity.

Remember to enjoy the view of the lake and surrounding mountains as you continue your round at Two Eagles.

Photograph by Stephanie Tracey of Photography West, Kelowna

BLACK MOUNTAIN
Golf Club

PAR 4 ◆ 363 YARDS

Kelowna, BC
250.765.6890
www.blackmountaingolf.ca

From the moment you arrive at Black Mountain Golf Club in Kelowna, you can clearly see that it is a unique facility. With the male staff wearing Loudmouth golf pants and the female staff wearing short shorts, Black Mountain is all about providing a fun and relaxed golf experience. The Wayne Carleton design on this scenic 6,394-yard course epitomizes the club's attitude toward the game, as the layout is fun to play every step of the way. The first hole gets the party started.

Set in the mountains a half hour from Big White Ski Resort, Black Mountain is a visual delight. Four tee boxes set up the beautiful par 4 from 234 yards back to 363 yards. The tees are elevated and the landing area generous, allowing for plenty of options off

the tee to get the round going. A large fairway bunker on the left encourages ideal tee shots down the right center.

The green is above the fairway, making approach shots about a club and a half longer than the yardage. The large putting surface is two-tiered, protected by two bunkers on the left and one on the back right. With a false front, shots coming up a little short will roll back off. It's all part of the fun.

Photograph by Colin Jewall

BLACK MOUNTAIN
Golf Club

PAR 4 ◆ 372 YARDS

Kelowna, BC
250.765.6890
www.blackmountaingolf.ca

Island greens present one of the most exciting, and fun, shots in golf. Most of them around the world are on par 3s. Architect Wayne Carleton created something a little different and very special at Black Mountain Golf Club. The stunningly beautiful fifth hole features an island green, but this terrific hole is a par 4.

The challenge off the tee is to hit a drive that will leave a second shot that can be stopped on the island. Water traces the right side before cutting across at the end of the fairway, making left centre the best target. The 150-yard marker is a very good aiming point but be aware that the ball carries farther at Black Mountain's elevation. There is a pot bunker on the water's edge, 90 yards from the hazard-riddled green.

While water surrounds it, the green is also guarded by a large bunker front right and a smaller one behind the putting surface. However, the green is large and receptive as it slopes back to front—Carleton's way of keeping this one of the most challenging, unique, and exciting holes on the course.

Photograph by Colin Jewall

45

CANOE CREEK
Golf Course

10 HOLE

PAR 4 ◆ 377 YARDS

Salmon Arm, BC
866.431.3285
www.canoecreekgolf.com

Incorporating the natural waterway that gave Canoe Creek Golf Course its name, the 10th hole is arguably the most picturesque. Water all but surrounds the green, which is accessed by way of a stone slab over the creek, and meanders down the right side of the fairway in a series of rock-edged pools. The challenges here are not contrived, but rather the natural result of the shape of the land and the flow of the water.

The hole is uphill all the way, requiring an extra club or even two off the tee, and the fairway is comparatively narrow with the area directly in front of the elevated green severely constricted.

The left side is well-treed and features the tall fescue and uncut rough that recur throughout the beautifully maintained course; the feeling is distinctly reminiscent of a British Isles links-style track. The elevation change will also be a factor in club selection on your approach shot, where landing short may leave you in the water and going long may result in a downhill putt that will test your nerves and your finesse.

Photograph © hux.net

CANOE CREEK
Golf Course

15 HOLE

PAR 4 ◆ 375 YARDS

Salmon Arm, BC
866.431.3285
www.canoecreekgolf.com

The absence of bunkers on hole 15 at Canoe Creek Golf Course bestows a deceptive sense of security. The fairway bends slightly to the right around a stand of trees, and a stretch of pronounced rough runs the full length along the left. An errant shot can easily leave you in deep trouble, as the green is sited virtually within the marsh, with a very limited approach area. Canadian Golf Hall of Famer Dave Barr was instrumental in the design of the course, and nowhere is his influence more visible than in the design of the superb greens. Read the breaks carefully, as the subtleness of the slopes has resulted in many a three-putt.

As a whole, the course's layout exploits the region's natural attributes, which provide both defences and visual appeal. Mature trees, impeccable fairways, deep rough, waving fescue, and a rural feel reinforce the course's special character; it's a traditional look with a modern approach, sometimes challenging but always enjoyable.

Photograph © hux.net

COPPER POINT
Golf Club

18 HOLE

PAR 4 ◆ 406 YARDS

Invermere, BC
877.418.GOLF(4653)
www.copperpointgolf.com

The Columbia River Valley, bordered by the Canadian Rockies and the Purcell Mountains, is one of the most beautifully scenic areas in Canada. At Copper Point Golf Club, just a few miles north of the Columbia's headwaters, the unique and dramatic beauty is on display at every turn. The 18th hole is a picturesque and perfect example.

From the copper tees, 312 yards from the center of the green, you cross just a corner of the large pond that shapes the dogleg to the right. From the other three tee boxes, especially the back tees at 406 yards, you can decide how much of the dogleg you want to cut off after carrying your shot 250 yards over the water.

Past the Douglas firs on the right side and the pond, from the fairway you'll face a second shot of 150 yards or less to an elevated green with a narrow opening between massive bunkers. The putting surface is 60 feet deep, with a bowl-like contour that feeds shots into the centre of the green from the left and back.

The Purcells tower behind the tee boxes, and from the fairway and green the views of the Rocky Mountains are spectacular on Copper Point's grand finale.

Photograph by Blue Coconut Media

CROWN ISLE
Resort & Golf Community

3 HOLE

PAR 4 ◆ 425 YARDS

Courtenay, BC
888.338.8439
www.crownisle.com

Crown Isle Resort & Golf Community features a Graham Cooke and Associates-designed course as the jewel of a master-planned residential community. Eleven on-course lakes and a thoughtful combination of natural and planted vegetation are backed by panoramic views in any direction, including a striking prospect of the Comox Glacier.

One of only nine courses in British Columbia that is a certified Audubon Cooperative Sanctuary, Crown Isle is home to various birds, including resident bald eagles that can be seen throughout the year, as well as numerous migratory species that return to the lakes as primary nesting areas.

The par-4 third is an ideal hole to showcase the skills of the long hitter but beware the risks if a shot is slightly off target. At 425 yards, the dogleg left has water from tee to green along the right side and out of bounds down the left. Three bunkers, two on the left and one on the right, mark the bend in the fairway, but a well-placed tee shot will find ample landing room between the bunkers and a 180-yard shot to a kidney-shaped green.

If the winds are blowing, the golfer must account for the gusts because the three bunkers that guard the green will easily swallow any errant shot. The pin position will require shot-making at its best. If situated at the front, the green provides a fairly level approach. Further back, however, the pin can be located on the upper shelf of the two-tiered green; balls that do not rest on the level portion will roll off the sides, making for a somewhat difficult return putt to the elevated pin placement.

Photograph by Crown Isle Resort & Golf Community

FAIRVIEW MOUNTAIN
Golf Club

18 HOLE

PAR 4 ◆ 468 YARDS

Oliver, BC
250.498.6050
www.fairviewmountain.com

On the mountainside above the city of Oliver, better known as the wine capital of Canada, Fairview Mountain Golf Club commands majestic views of the spectacular Okanagan Valley. Formed in 1925, the club has gracefully evolved into one of the country's top-rated courses. Les Furber designed the current 18-hole, 7,025-yard layout in 1990 with wide fairways and challenging green complexes. All the scenic and pure golf aspects of Fairview Mountain are on display on the 18th hole.

From the elevated tee box more than 70 feet above the fairway on the 468-yard hole, the valley stretches into the distance past the rows of grapevines of the winery Fairview Cellars. Like all the other holes at Fairview Mountain, no houses are in sight, simply the natural beauty of the Okanagan. There is almost always some wind blowing, from either the left or right, adding to the challenge. When it's from the left,

the out-of-bounds stakes along the right side get your attention from the back tees and all the way up to the forward tees at 425 yards.

The ideal tee shot is about 250 yards with a slight right-to-left ball flight, leaving a mid-iron to 8-iron into a well-protected green. A long bunker traces the entire left side and curls around the back, and a smaller bunker guards the right. A spine runs through the middle of the green, creating two tiers on this challenging and fitting finale to an exceptional course.

Photograph by Gord Wylie

GOLDEN
Golden Club

PAR 4 ◆ 378 YARDS

Golden, BC
250.344.2700
www.golfgolden.com

Golden Golf Club is one of the most visually appealing courses in the game. At 2,590 feet above sea level and with Kicking Horse Mountain, the Canadian Rockies, Mount Seven, Holt Creek, and the mighty Columbia River as design elements, it's incomparable.

Architect Bill Newis designed the terrific front nine in 1986, and Les Furber added the back in 1996 to complete the 6,825-yard, par-72 layout. Fittingly, the 11th has become the club's signature hole. Holt Creek tumbles and gurgles to the right of the tee boxes and traces that side of the fairway before crossing it in front of the green. From the elevated tees, you can see the green in the distance just slightly to the right, the Columbia River straight ahead, and Mount Seven defining the horizon. The gold tees play 378 yards, the whites 356, and the reds 307.

With the 150-yard marker the target, the ideal tee shot is 210 yards from the whites, 230 from the golds. That leaves a downhill mid- to short-iron shot over Holt Creek to a green nestled against the mountainside on the right and trees in the back. A pot bunker two paces from the front and a bunker front-right protect the deceptive, mounded green.

The 11th is a classic par 4 on a spectacular course. With no out of bounds, and plenty of wildlife, Golden Golf Club is an unforgettable natural beauty.

Photographs: above by Don Weixl; facing page by Cheryl Chapman

HIGHLAND PACIFIC
Golf Course

5 HOLE

PAR 4 ♦ 378 YARDS

Victoria, BC
250.478.GOLF(4653)
www.highlandpacificgolf.com

Highland Pacific Golf Course's lush fairways thread through a majestic landscape of forest, rock, fescue, and natural water features. After opening 18 holes in 2010, it has become a must-play in Victoria, whether you play the whole golf course from 6,603 yards, or decide you might have more fun from a shorter distance. Its driving range features a two-tiered tee line of covered and heated stalls, long and short game practice areas, lights for evening practice, and real terrain targets.

The fifth hole is the definition of a short, tough par 4. The view from the tee is spectacular with the Olympic Mountains in the distance, but don't be drawn in. You must hit two very precise shots to hit this green in regulation.

Off the tee, the ideal drive will have you targeting the 150-yard marker; go too far and your ball will land either on a downward slope or in the water. On the left side sits a well-located bunker that you want to avoid.

Club selection is key for the second shot since it requires a one- or two-club difference to the elevated green surface, which looks very small from 150 yards out. Many golfers under-club and will find the bunker on the right side; any ball hit right of that could easily disappear because of the 50-yard drop to the water below. A bailout area left of the green's surface is the decision for many golfers who are unsure of wind conditions and their shot-making ability. Birdies are always possible, but it's probably best to take your par and run.

Photograph by Rob Perry

KOKANEE SPRINGS
Resort Club

PAR 4 ◆ 400 YARDS

Crawford Bay, BC
800.979.7999
www.kokaneesprings.com

Renowned architect Norman Woods created a timeless layout back in 1968 at Kokanee Springs Resort Club that, with a recent multimillion-dollar refurbishment, not only stands the test of time but also improves with each passing season. The 14th hole, a par 4, is a classic example of the deft Woods touch as natural beauty plays a key role in its charm and challenge.

Called "The Peninsula" for the way the tee juts out into a pond, the 14th demands strategy from each of the four tee boxes. From the back tees at 400 yards, and from the 371-yard blues and the 358-yard whites, the first shot must carry the pond. The reds are to the left and past the water hazard. However, from each tee, the challenge is the same—place the tee shot to set up a safe approach to the green. Majestic 200-year-old cedars guard both sides of the narrow entrance, making second shots from right or left daunting.

Two large bunkers protect the front of the long, thin green that deceptively runs back to front. A distinctive rock wall lines the front right bunker, edging the eminently playable sand blended specifically for the 66 bunkers on the course. The Hazel May Basin forms a lush backdrop to the tall cedars ringing the green, typical of the astounding views—including the Kokanee Glacier—throughout this 6,604-yard gem.

Photograph by Don Weixl

MORGAN CREEK
Golf Course

9 HOLE

PAR 4 ◆ 442 YARDS

Surrey, BC
604.531.GOLF(4653)
www.morgancreekgolf.com

When Tom McBroom, one of Canada's leading course architects, crafted Morgan Creek Golf Club from the natural contours of the land, a spectacular course was sure to follow, given its surroundings of breathtaking Mount Baker and the rugged Golden Ears Mountain Range. Strategic bunkering and natural water features make the course both scenic and memorable no matter what time of year you play.

Named "Golf Facility of the Year" by the PGA of British Columbia in 2008 and listed as one of *Golf Digest*'s "Places to Play," the 18-hole, 6,900-yard beauty impresses golfers of all levels. Players far and wide are attracted to the course's location in Surrey, just 30 minutes from the heart of Vancouver and 10 minutes from the international border at Blaine, Washington.

Whether playing from the black tee of hole 9—442 yards to the green—or the shorter red teeing ground, all golfers will enjoy this challenge. A good tee shot on the tree-lined par-4 hole will send you to the left side of an expansive and receptive fairway; too far right and you are faced with a full carry, over water, to a two-tiered, kidney-shaped green.

From the fairway's left side, a slight fade will find you targeting the back of the green. At the front, a depression on the left would require a delicate chip shot to avoid watching your ball roll with the strong left-to-right incline into the pond. Regardless of your exact placement, every shot is a reminder that accuracy is your best friend. Morgan Creek is truly a great golf experience—from tee to green.

Photograph by John Johnson

NICKLAUS NORTH
Golf Course

18 HOLE

PAR 4 ♦ 450 YARDS

Whistler, BC
800.386.9898
www.nicklausnorth.com

A great course requires a great finishing hole, and architect Jack Nicklaus follows through beautifully at Nicklaus North Golf Course. The 18th demands length and accuracy from all five tee boxes that stretch the hole from 266 yards all the way back to 450 yards.

The fairway carves a straight and fairly generous path, but is bordered on each side by trees and natural areas. Stray drives left or right dim any hopes of a strong finish. Shots in to the green must first carry Fitzsimmons Creek, which rumbles across the width of the fairway with the runoff from Whistler and Blackcomb Mountains on its way across the 16th hole and finally to Green Lake. The hole is slightly uphill and usually plays into the prevailing wind, so laying up in front of the creek can be a thoughtful option.

Whether it is a second or third, the shot over the creek is beautifully framed by 80-foot trees guarding the entrance. Greg Norman captured the 1997 Canadian Skins Game in a playoff on 18 by hitting a 191-yard 5-iron from the fairway bunker to eight feet for his birdie. The well-protected green, with a huge, deep horseshoe-shaped bunker front left and a large one guarding the right side, is big and wide with mounding along the right. The Shark's great shot aside, par is a wonderful score on this fitting finale to Nicklaus' Whistler masterpiece.

Photograph by John Henebry

NORTHLANDS
Golf Course

PAR 4 ◆ 398 YARDS

North Vancouver, BC
604.924.2950
www.golfnorthlands.com

First-time visitors find it hard to believe that Northlands Golf Course is a municipal course, because it feels like a private facility. Owned and operated by the District of North Vancouver, it is considered one of metro Vancouver's most challenging. Les Furber designed the 398-yard first hole as an attention grabber, equally scenic and complex, a perfect introduction to the course, which demands that you arrive ready to play.

With water approximately 200 yards to your left and a narrow landing area to your right, it naturally causes a bit of hesitation. Players hitting a low- to mid-iron tee shot will find themselves safe but facing a difficult second shot: a downhill lie hitting to an elevated green. Players pulling out their three-wood or driver, if successful, will have a great chance to hit the green in regulation due to the flat lie and proximity to the green. The staff tip: grip it and rip it. Once on the two-tiered green, it can easily

be a three-putt if you are not positioned below the hole. A bogey is not uncommon, so making par or a birdie will definitely give you the satisfaction and confidence to venture on.

Open for 18-hole play since 1997, the course presents a well-formulated mix of complicated holes, friendly scenic downhill vistas, and strategically located hazards. Suited to all levels, each hole has four sets of tees and the greens are generous and relatively level. The Northlands experience is further enhanced by the unspoiled feeling of the forested mountainside site.

Photographs by Pablo Su

NORTHLANDS
Golf Course

10 HOLE

PAR 4 ◆ 312 YARDS

North Vancouver, BC
604.924.2950
www.golfnorthlands.com

Letting out a sigh of relief after finishing the front nine at Northlands Golf Course is well deserved. And now the 10th hole looks simple enough. A 312-yard downhill par 4: What is so difficult about that? Well, let's just say that you do not have to be long to be tough.

Your tee shot is vital on this hole. Hitting it too far will put you right into the pond. Hit it too short and you find yourself wishing you had hit it too far. From high above, the green looks like a postage stamp surrounded by water. A 200-yard tee shot will leave you in a comfortable position to decide if you want to attack the flag or play safe and aim for the middle of the green. The middle is the best so that you can circumvent the water hazard as well as the bunker on the front right lip of the green.

Once the 10th hole is over, it's time to put your birdie hat on and make up some lost strokes. The next four holes will be quite enjoyable. Watch out for the 15th and 18th holes as you come in.

Photograph by Pablo Su

QUILCHENA
Golf and Country Club

PAR 4 ◆ 328 YARDS

Richmond, BC
604.277.1101
www.qgolfclub.ca

The course at Quilchena Golf and Country Club is designed to present the player with much more than just a physical challenge. Naturally, playing the course requires strength and accuracy, but the test reaches far beyond. In fact, the third hole, which won't necessarily intimidate golfers with its distance, will certainly bring into play the best of the game's mental challenges.

The pond along the left side of the fairway helps to shape the left-to-right dogleg. However, as much as players instinctively shy away from water to err on the side of safety, tee shots have to favor that side as tall trees guard the right side. A very well-designed short par 4, hole 3 requires players to carefully choose their club and direction to lay up to their preferred yardage for a second shot onto a gently sloped green.

The rest of Quilchena's 120 acres of natural beauty continue to set the standard for privacy, exclusivity, and service, enhancing the experience at every use of a club. Players could not ask for a finer course than this par-73 layout.

A course that taxes the full range of each player's skills is the culmination of the club's 15 charter members, who first brought their vision to fruition more than 85 years ago. Quilchena continues to be maintained by dedicated members and staff.

Photographs © hux.net

QUILCHENA
Golf and Country Club

12 HOLE

PAR 4 ◆ 390 YARDS

Richmond, BC
604.277.1101
www.qgolfclub.ca

Considered by many to be the best hole on the course for design, playability, and setting, Quilchena Golf and Country Club's number 12 delivers the ultimate contemporary golf experience.

Trees on both sides of the fairway make this hole look narrower than it plays, but don't relax too much. A large tree on the left and a group of trees, short and right of the green, block approaches to the green from errant tee shots. Going off line here can land you in real trouble.

Even from the fairway, the second shot is an exciting one. The small green is accessed through a restricted narrow opening, and the rest of the green is surrounded by water. Often a

pivotal hole, many friendly matches and tournaments swing on the twelfth.

Typical of the course's design and rich, natural surroundings, the hole makes it easy to forget the city is just minutes away. Quilchena is truly a restorative retreat from hectic daily life, and every hole contributes to its identity as "a world apart."

Photograph © hux.net

THE REDWOODS

Golf Course

Langley, BC
604.882.5132
www.redwoods-golf.com

As you step up to the first tee for a great day on the course, pause to take in the ambience: fairways surrounded by large trees and, in the background, a panoramic view of British Columbia's Coastal Mountains.

The Redwoods opened in 1994 and takes its name from the 38 hundred-year-old heritage California redwoods that border the north end of the property. A Ted Locke design located just 30 minutes east of Vancouver, the 6,500-yard masterpiece situated in rolling countryside and forested terrain is a dynamic work of art.

At 319 yards, the 10th hole is an inspiring example of Locke's design; it's not the longest par 4 on the course, but its diverse features will challenge the full spectrum of any player's ability. Off the tee, a golfer faces many decisions with club selection for a strategic ball placement. The narrow, slightly downhill dogleg will entice the challenger to drive the corner as the fairway widens 200 yards out. However, a miss could result in an unfavourable ball position; the safe play will be on the left side toward the target fairway bunkers.

As the golfer rounds the corner, a stunning view over the undulating green masks a deceptive target. Landing an accurate approach safely on the green will avoid three bunkers—one left and two behind, not to mention a narrow, rocky creek that wraps itself around the front edge.

Photograph by Rob Perry

THE RIDGE
at Copper Point

PAR 4 ◆ 397 YARDS

Invermere, BC
877.418.GOLF(4653)
www.copperpointgolf.com

The Ridge at Copper Point is as unique as it is scenic. Though playing to just over 5,000 yards, it is not a short golf course. The Ridge has 10 full-length par 3s ranging from 147 to 241 yards, eight par 4s ranging from 324 to 463 yards, and no par 5s. Players enjoy a complete golf experience on a course manicured to championship conditions and can complete play in three hours. The 14th hole on The Ridge is a beautiful example.

From the elevated tee boxes, the Canadian Rockies are on the right and the spectacular Columbia River Valley is located to the west. From the back tee box, a drive of 240 yards is ideal to a landing area that narrows 150 yards from the green. Trees line the left side of the hole and a large pond that stretches along the right almost to the green directs you to the target.

The wide but narrow green—60 feet by 30 feet—is slightly elevated and protected by three big, white silica sand bunkers on the right side. The tiered putting surface, with a back shelf, sits beside a stand of Douglas firs in an idyllic Columbia Valley setting.

Photograph by Blue Coconut Media

RIVERSHORE ESTATES

and Golf Links

PAR 4 ◆ 402 YARDS

Kamloops, BC
250.573.4211
www.rivershoregolflinks.com

Although the beautiful setting of rugged hills and tall fescue is most reminiscent of links golf, a lake defines the entire left side of the 10th hole at Rivershore Estates and Golf Links, just east of Kamloops. A master at incorporating natural elements, architect Robert Trent Jones used the water, a stand of trees, and natural mounds to create this challenging and visually stunning par 4.

Laying parallel to the South Thompson River, the 10th plays either downwind or into the wind. With the green a distant goal at the end of the lake—402 yards from the back tees—and the wind, proper club selection and placement of the tee shot are crucial. A stand of trees guards the right side at just over 200 yards. A series of three fescue-covered hillocks beyond the trees reinforce Jones' encouragement of a layup shot between the trees and the lake. The fairway is barely 30 yards wide in the landing area, demanding a precise tee shot.

The ideal drive leaves a second shot over the lake of 120 to 140 yards. Jones thoughtfully provided a relatively flat green of more than 6,000 square feet for that intimidating shot and sloped it gently back to front. On the left, he carved two massive bunkers into the mound than runs behind the green and added another large one on the right. At Rivershore's 10th, the view from the fairway is as dramatic as the shot to be played.

Photograph © hux.net

RIVERSHORE ESTATES
and Golf Links

16 HOLE

PAR 4 ◆ 388 YARDS

Kamloops, BC
250.573.4211
www.rivershoregolflinks.com

The mound that cradles the 10th green runs the entire length of the Rivershore Estates and Golf Links property and cuts across the 16th fairway, providing architect Robert Trent Jones with a wonderful design element. The lake that protects the front of the 10th green curls behind the mound to front the 16th green but is not visible from the tee. As he does throughout Rivershore, at the 388-yard 16th Jones encourages thoughtful and strategic golf.

The fairway is lined by fescue and sage, giving the par 4 a links feel, enhanced when wind blows across the hole from the left or the right. Tee shots should be played short of ledges created by the mound—ideally just under 240 yards from the tips—or the second shot will be off a severe downhill lie. A subtle challenge is the optical illusion from the fairway. It appears that the green is considerably below the fairway and so many players hit at least one less club. However, the green is barely six feet lower, resulting in numerous shots finding the lake.

The putting surface slopes back to front and is guarded by bunkers on both sides. The front of the green is just five steps from the water, making front pin positions very intimidating. Yet shots hit long to avoid the lake encounter a significant downslope toward that water. Jones created a classic short par 4 at the 16th.

Photograph © hux.net

THE CLUB AT SAGEBRUSH

9 HOLE

PAR 4 ◆ 442 YARDS

Quilchena, BC
877.350.9555
www.sagebrushclub.com

Mirroring and blending with its expansive surroundings, The Club at Sagebrush offers a transcendent golf experience as timeless as the game itself.

On a stunning 389-acre site within the historic, 100,000-acre Quilchena Ranch in British Columbia's scenic Nicola Valley is one of the most distinctive and unique golf courses anywhere. Evoking the game's cherished heritage, co-designers Rod Whitman, Richard Zokol, and Armen Suny created a masterpiece, the first in Canada to boast modern minimalist style that plays the way golf is meant to be played—firm and fast. Paying homage to the game's roots, there are no rakes in the bunkers or markers on the tee boxes; the player with the honour decides the group's teeing spot, and rather than a par, holes are assigned a Standard Scratch Score (SSS).

The notorious ninth hole measures 254 yards from its most forward tee to 442 yards for the most advanced players, and has an SSS of 4. Sagebrush's rugged natural beauty is on full display at this slightly uphill straightway hole, Nicola Lake shimmering in the background. The mound left of the fairway and the huge, rough-hewn bunker on the right narrow the landing area at 220 yards. Hitting a driver is enticing but risky. A lay up to short iron range is much wiser as the enourmous green—fully 17,000 square feet—features dramatic undulations that horseshoe around a bunker on the left. The hole simply requires keen awareness, intuition, creativity, and a love of the game: essential elements of a round at Sagebrush.

Photograph © hux.net

THE CLUB AT SAGEBRUSH

13 HOLE

PAR 4 ◆ 320 YARDS

Quilchena, BC
877.350.9555
www.sagebrushclub.com

One of the most alluring and enjoyable features of a great golf course is a driveable par 4. The 13th hole at The Club at Sagebrush is a classic example. Since opening day in 2009, very few golfers have stood on any of the four tee boxes and looked down toward the large green—178 yards from the most forward tee, 320 from the championship tee—and not reached for their driver.

Inspired by the world-renowned par-4 10th at Riviera Country Club, the 13th at Sagebrush irresistibly invites players to test their ability to drive the green perched behind a massive bunker. The wide-open corridor to the left, bounded by the forested hillside, makes going for it enticing while simultaneously demanding that the well-executed tee shots must come perilously close to the course's boundary to gain the best angle to the hole. Perfectly struck drives to the slope in front of the trees will bound toward the green, perhaps even reach it.

On the other hand, the more defensive tee shots to the expansive area on the right force players to deal with a very tricky second shot over the ominous bunker to a green sloping away from them to the back. The lip of this ancient-looking hazard guarding almost the entire front of the green increases in height and complexity the further right the player finds his or her line of play.

Beautiful, exciting, driveable—the 13th at Sagebrush yields many eagles, birdies, and pars, and lots of others.

Photograph © hux.net

THE CLUB AT SAGEBRUSH

PAR 4 ◆ 434 YARDS

Quilchena, BC
877.350.9555
www.sagebrushclub.com

Golf writer and author Lorne Rubenstein's eloquent description captures the essence of The Club at Sagebrush: "Sagebrush reaches into, explores, and touches golf's soul. To play the course is to experience the generosity of spirit that one finds at the Old Course, Royal Melbourne, and Muirfield. Sagebrush embodies traditional values that golf at its best and most exhilarating represents. The open expanse allows the golfer to experience freedom, while inviting a wide variety of shots to answer Sagebrush's questions. To play Sagebrush is to uncover one's golfing mind, in a setting that encourages discovery from the first to the final shot."

With its massive firm and fast fairways, rough-edged blowout-style bunkers, and enourmous undulating putting surfaces, Sagebrush creates a singular feeling of being in touch with the game and its history. On every hole, in every playing condition, players are limited only by their own imagination.

The stark natural beauty and the traditional elements of this modern minimalist design are on full panoramic display from the 17th hole's four tee boxes. The natural rolls of the fairway, the fescue and sage-edged bunkers, and the 18th hole and beautiful Nicola Lake in the background combine to provide one of the most captivating looks in golf. The beautiful combination of finishing holes is aptly known as "Coming Home," a feeling golfers from around the world experience when they play Sagebrush, which has been named best new course in Canada by *Golf Digest* and *SCOREGolf* magazines and has been recognized as the eighth-best modern course in Canada by *Golfweek* magazine.

Photograph © hux.net

SALMON ARM
Golf Club

PAR 4 ◆ 407 YARDS

Salmon Arm, BC
250.832.3667
www.salmonarmgolf.com

Les Furber made great use of what nature provided when laying out Salmon Arm Golf Club's 407-yard 11th hole. The first glance can only be described as breathtaking.

From an elevated tee box, the entire tree-lined hole comes into view. Be sure to navigate away from the long, deep gully that interrupts the tree line on the left, where errant tee shots are destined to be gobbled up. The real strategy to playing the hole emanates from the 200-foot-tall Douglas fir that must be negotiated on the second shot to an elevated, narrow two-tier green. Tee shots left short of this tree will force you to play over the entire expanse of the scrub pine and fescue-filled gully to reach the green; tee shots not long enough will require second shots to be curved to the left or right around the imposing tree.

The green's considerable elevation change between the two tiers puts a premium on being on the correct tier when making the approach.

Overcompensating to avoid one hazard on this hole will bring you hard against another. No matter your journey or score, this is one hole you will remember.

Photograph © hux.net

SANDPIPER
Golf Resort

PAR 4 ◆ 361 YARDS

Harrison Mills, BC
877.796.1001
www.sandpiperresort.ca

Nestled in a centuries-old forest along the blue-green waters of the Harrison River in Fraser Valley, Sandpiper Golf Resort is an outstanding escape. Featuring gently sloped fairways and four sets of tees, the course is playable by all. Russ Olson's design takes full advantage of the scenery, which is so breathtaking that you might actually find it distracting during your first round.

The par-72 course runs 6,500 yards, with challenges diverse enough to exercise the full spectrum of a player's skills. It is also home to a notable bed-and-breakfast: Rowena's Inn On the River, secluded on a lush 160-acre estate complete with its own private air strip that laterally straddles the 17th hole.

At 361 yards, the 5th hole is not the longest par 4 on the course, but its unique features will force you to rise to the occasion of mastering it. The first difficulty stems from a substantial drop in elevation, always a test in selecting clubs and judging the correct landing area off the tee. Then, the fairway is constricted by two bunkers about 250 yards out. Shaped like a kidney, the right bunker sits on the direct line from tee to green, with a tall birch in the middle. The tree makes you want to aim left, but don't do it. The better shot is to fade right toward the green, which has an undulating profile and sits in a "catcher's mitt" of 120-foot-tall Douglas firs and cedars. Placing the ball safely on the green will allow you to avoid the trees and rough surroundings on three sides.

Photograph by Doug Johnson

SHAUGHNESSY
Golf and Country Club

PAR 4 ◆ 421 YARDS

Vancouver, BC
604.266.4141
www.shaughnessy.org

The iconic A.V. Macan masterpiece opened in 1960 and has been considered one of the game's finest courses ever since. On 162 acres of gently rolling parkland leased from the Musqueam Band, Shaughnessy Golf and Country Club traces the edge of the Fraser River defined by more than 150 species of trees, some firs and cedars more than 200 years old. The club itself celebrated its centenary in 2011, and the 7,010-yard course has hosted three Canadian Open championships.

Because of Macan's classic design of tree-lined narrow fairways, well-placed bunkers, and small greens, accuracy—not length—is the key to playing well at Shaughnessy. A par 4, the ninth hole is a fine example of Macan's art.

The tee shot is slightly uphill on the gentle dogleg left. In the landing area, the fairway bottlenecks 270 yards off the back tees, narrowed by a fairway bunker on the right and tall sequoia on the left. In the 2011 Canadian Open, the game's finest players hit tee shots short of the narrowing, leaving themselves second shots of just under 200 yards.

The Fraser River and Georgia Strait in the distance come into view near the green that is guarded by a large bunker on the right stretching almost the length of the putting surface, and a smaller bunker front left. Unfelt wind off the river, the slight elevation, and slope of the green front-to-back make par a fine score for both professionals and amateurs—just as Macan planned it.

Photograph by Margaret Barr

SHAUGHNESSY
Golf and Country Club

HOLE 14

PAR 4 ◆ 315 YARDS

Vancouver, BC
604.266.4141
www.shaughnessy.org

A short par 4 is one of the most exciting and challenging types of holes in the game. Shaughnessy Golf and Country Club's 14th hole is one of the finest examples. Architect A.V. Macan built in an ingenious variety of elements to create a classic risk/reward test.

From all five tee boxes—the championship tee is at 315 yards, the red tee at 287 yards—you have two options: Attempt to drive the green, getting the ball as close to the green as possible, or lay up to your ideal distance for a second shot. The risk in attempting to drive the green is that the fairway is very narrow in front of the green, only about 12 paces wide. And the green, which slopes front to back, is well protected by bunkers on both sides. The putting surface itself is narrow, with a ridge making it almost two-tiered; it's difficult to hold pitch shots if drives miss left or right. During the 2005 and 2011 Canadian Opens, the majority of the pros went for the green.

If you lay up and hit a tee shot of 180 to 200 yards, you have to land in the left-center of the fairway. Be wary of tall trees on the right side 70 yards from the green and two fairway bunkers on the left side. You can make a birdie, but don't be surprised if you make bogey.

Photograph by Margaret Barr

SHAUGHNESSY
Golf and Country Club

16 HOLE

PAR 4 ♦ 372 YARDS

Vancouver, BC
604.266.4141
www.shaughnessy.org

Architect A.V. Macan's subtle insistence on accuracy and strategy is elegantly demonstrated at Shaughnessy Golf and Country Club's 16th hole. On most modern layouts, a par 4 of less than 400 yards is an invitation to hit the driver as hard and long as possible. At Shaughnessy, Macan gives pros and recreational players alike cause to pause and think about club selection, whether from the red tees at 314 yards or from the championship tees at 372 yards.

The hole slightly turns to the right, but at that gentle corner 100 yards from the green two fairway bunkers on the right and one on the left pinch the landing area. The narrowness of the opening between the bunkers encourages most players to lay up, ideally leaving about a 130-yard second shot.

Even from that range, the second shot into the 16th is challenging. The green is elongated and slopes front to back and to the left at the narrow front. The pin position is key to club selection—the left front is especially difficult to hold—and a pot bunker front right, a large bunker back right, and another front left protect the green well.

The hole is straightforward. Macan puts it all out front and lets you decide how to take up the challenge.

Photograph by Margaret Barr

TALKING ROCK
Golf Course & Quaaout Lodge

14 HOLE

PAR 4 ◆ 361 YARDS

Chase, BC
800.663.4303
www.quaaoutlodge.com

Certain holes provide a special opportunity that ardent golfers seek, a chance to walk that fine line between success and disaster. Talking Rock Golf Course & Quaaout Lodge's course architects Cooke and Carleton made sure that the relatively short 14th delivers on that promise. Strike the right note and it offers a real chance for birdies, but don't be fooled; it can certainly be challenging. Errant shots easily land you in trouble, with double bogeys a very real possibility.

With its slight dogleg right and an uphill approach to a narrow green, the hole looks simple to play from the tee box. A fairway wood or long iron here is the smart play. Three bunkers lining the left side of the fairway await any ball that overshoots the mark on the dogleg. Finding the fairway is crucial to setting up an uphill approach shot to the green that is divided by a center ridge. If the flag is to the front, be wary of the sloping hillside just short of the fringe. Playing a little more club on this hole is ideal, as short shots will face a difficult up and down.

Stands of pine and fir with a mountain vista backing the green make you feel as if you are alone in a private forest clearing. Not just a treat for the eye, hole 14 is a pleasure to play as well, no matter your handicap.

Photograph © hux.net

BOOTLEG GAP Golf

PAR 3 ◆ 193 YARDS

Kimberley, BC
250.427.7077
www.bootleggapgolf.com

Once the home of the famous Sullivan Mine, Kimberley, British Columbia, has become a hub of world-class golfing, skiing, hiking, biking, and fly fishing, with a distinct Bavarian flair from the European miner influence of the past. Amidst this charming atmosphere is Bootleg Gap Golf's signature par-3 12th hole.

One of 27 holes at the public Furber-designed course, the 12th offers a dramatic 193-yard dive along a hoodoo rock formation and is the first of three holes rimming the beautiful St. Mary's River, a stretch that is sure to restore the spirit, even as it tests the skill.

An elevated tee box, usually affected by crosswinds, leads to a well-protected green 50 feet below. If you judged wind direction and speed correctly, you'll be rewarded with a sense of accomplishment as the ball softly lands on the green between an array of bunkers large and small, away from a rough treed slope that sits just off the back edge. Club selection is more critical than ever here, making for a great risk/reward experience.

The other 17 holes of the championship course, which is suitable for all levels, combine spacious fairways with a few tighter riverside holes where accuracy is at a premium. The Rec-9 track, ideal for beginners or casual players, is a beautifully maintained hybrid course with a collection of par 3s, 4s, and a great 5. Bootleg Gap Golf also has one of the best practice facilities in the region. In the background, beautiful vistas of Bootleg and Pudding Burn Mountains make both these facilities particularly scenic.

Photograph by Don Weixl

CANOE CREEK
Golf Course

PAR 3 ◆ 170 YARDS

Salmon Arm, BC
866.431.3285
www.canoecreekgolf.com

There is good reason why number 3 is considered the signature hole at Canoe Creek Golf Course. First and foremost, it is truly beautiful, featuring a cascading waterfall, sparkling fountain, and lush vegetation. The contrast between flawlessly groomed playing surfaces and surrounding natural growth is clearly evident on this hole and throughout the course.

Canoe Creek offers five sets of tees throughout, inviting both the novice golfer and the accomplished player to enjoy the spectacular course's risks and rewards. At just 170 yards from the championship tees, hole 3 relies on tight spaces and lots of water for its considerable challenge. The deep pot bunkers that are characteristic of the course can also be found guarding the immaculate, subtly undulating green. Accuracy rather than power is the key here. The elevation change indicates one less club off the tee than the distance alone would suggest, and any error to the right is almost certain to be promptly punished.

Photograph © hux.net

CRANBROOK
Golf Club

PAR 3 ◆ 195 YARDS

Cranbrook, BC
250.426.7812
www.golfcranbrook.com

Tucked away in the Kootenay Rockies, within the limits of the town of Cranbrook, the region's hub, is a special course just waiting to surprise. Mature trees maintain a lush parkland feel throughout a course that has something to offer every golfer, regardless of skill level or experience. Cranbrook Golf Club, a "player's course" in the fullest sense, was designed by its members. Over the past 20 years, it has been recognized for excellence within the golf community and selected to host numerous provincial and national championships. From grassroots beginnings—members with rakes and shovels—to a national standing as a respected and challenging course, Cranbrook's story has been a remarkable journey.

The 17th hole provides a good glimpse into the character of the course. At 195 yards, this can be an easy three or rapidly turn into a double bogey. The layout is fairly straightforward, relatively flat with a little increase in elevation from the front to the rear of the green.

You'll want to be on target here; water guards the left side of the green, with a substantial bunker on the right. Pin placement is absolutely key in determining your club selection. When the pin is placed in the left rear quadrant of the green, stretching to place your tee shot close to the pin has you flirting with the water. Taking a more conservative approach will leave you with a long, fairly challenging putt.

Simple par 3 indeed! Coming near the end of your day, losing concentration here can turn a good round into a disappointing round in no time at all.

Photograph by Steve Donaldson

FAIRWINDS
Golf Club

2 HOLE

PAR 3 ◆ 206 YARDS

Nanoose Bay, BC
888.781.2777
www.fairwinds.ca

Part of a master-planned, oceanfront community on Vancouver Island, the award-winning Fairwinds Golf Club is all about the social aspect of the game and is ideal for year-round play because of the region's mild climate. Its Furber design and pristine surroundings complement the many amenities and natural attributes of the area. Hole 2 ably captures the ambience of the 6,200-yard, par-71 course.

Standing on the elevated tee with spectacular vistas of the Coast Mountain Range on the mainland and ocean waters of Juan de Fuca Straight, the downhill par 3 is a joy to behold. Established stands of trees lining the fairways play with light and shadow, adding to the challenge of gauging distance and placing your shot.

The ideal shot ends at a green protected on the right and the back by a water hazard that wraps around two-thirds of its circumference yet is practically invisible from the tee. Short is definitely better than long in this case. The front left bunker guards a portion of the green that cannot be seen from the tee. With wind that seems to be ever-present, this memorable hole will have you coming back for the challenge time and again.

Photograph courtesy of Fairwinds Golf Club

FURRY CREEK
Golf & Country Club

14 HOLE

PAR 3 ◆ 211 YARDS

Furry Creek, BC
888.922.9462
www.furrycreekgolf.com

For sheer drama and natural beauty, few par 3 holes anywhere can match Furry Creek Golf & Country Club's 14th. One of the most picturesque, and most photographed, golf holes in British Columbia stretching into the deep blue waters of Howe Sound, it is defined by the rocky shore and glistening bunkers, framed by a backdrop of mountains.

Aptly nicknamed "Tee to Sea," the 14th requires a precise shot from the gold tee box 211 yards to the peninsula green that must first carry 175 yards over water, beach, and rocks. There is a generous bailout area to the right of the green, but the best result for any shot to the left would be landing in the 760-square-foot bunker tracing the front left of the green, or the 310-square-foot trap on the back left guarding the sound.

The long and narrow green encompasses more than 4,200 square feet. There is almost always some wind off the sound, making both the white tee box that can vary from 155 to 190 yards and the red tee box at 141 yards attractive options.

The Robert Muir Graves design offers remarkable mountain and sea views throughout the course, but the 14th—a full 357 feet below the clubhouse and the Sea to Sky Grill—is a quintessential BC panorama that you'll never forget.

Photographs by Rob Perry

GREYWOLF
Golf Course

6 HOLE

PAR 3 ◆ 200 YARDS

Panorama, BC
250.341.4100
888.473.9965
www.greywolfgolf.com

Rarely do courses fit so perfectly with the terrain that it seems that the land was just patiently waiting through the millennia for them to be built. Greywolf Golf Course is such a course. Architect Doug Carrick created this 7,140-yard mountain masterpiece by matching astounding views with shot values and playability every unforgettable step of the way. He saved his best for hole 6, which he envisioned when he first walked amid the towering pines and mountains.

Carrick's spectacular par 3 is aptly named "Cliffhanger." In the shadows of the Canadian Rockies, with tree-covered mountain slopes as a background and the jagged peaks of the Purcell Mountains creating a majestic horizon, the green is perched on the cliff's edge, 150 feet above the Toby Creek Valley. To the west stretches Hopeful Canyon. From any of the distinctly separate tees, which range from 77 yards to 200 yards to offer as much hope as you need, the mountains and the yawning canyon create an optical illusion.

The sixth green is actually massive, the second largest on the course at 7,500 square feet. In different circumstances, the large green with two bunkers in front and the surrounding apron of rough would hardly be intimidating. But in this quintessentially BC setting, Cliffhanger is very intimidating, and by any measure, one of the finest par 3s in golf.

Photograph by Dani Tchudin

111

THE HARVEST
Golf Club

16 HOLE

PAR 3 • 186 YARDS

Kelowna, BC
800.257.8577
www.harvestgolf.com

There is not a more aptly named course in golf than The Harvest Golf Club. The brilliant design by Graham Cooke takes full advantage of a remarkable 251-acre setting in East Kelowna above Okanagan Lake. Golfers can harvest samples from the surrounding 45 acres of orchards and vineyards, which adds to the club's unique charm.

With the look and feel of an inviting farmhouse, the clubhouse boasts views of the city, lake, and the rolling Cascade Mountains. Through welcoming fairways from every tee, Cooke gradually challenges the better players as they get closer to the green on a course where walking is always an option.

The 16th is the centerpiece of The Harvest's dramatic, and scenic, finishing holes. The par 3 can be played at 127 yards or from tee boxes stretching back to 186 yards. The views might distract you from noticing the hint of bunkers to the right of the green, but you'll definitely see the two large front left bunkers: the first 10 yards short of the green, the next hugging it. If the pin is in the front, the bowl shape might feed tee shots toward the hole. If the pin is on the back upper tier, par is a fine score.

Photograph courtesy of The Harvest Golf Club

HIGHLAND PACIFIC
Golf Course

8 HOLE

PAR 3 ◆ 221 YARDS

Victoria, BC
250.478.GOLF(4653)
www.highlandpacificgolf.com

Carved from the rolling landscape of the British Columbia wilderness, Victoria's Highland Pacific Golf Course was created for golfers who want to enjoy a scenic, challenging championship course that is playable year-round. Views of the majestic Olympic Mountains and the Strait of Juan de Fuca alone are enough to distract you, but this course has many other surprises in store.

Highland Pacific's lush fairways thread through a majestic landscape of forest, rock, fescue, and natural water features. With wide, sweeping fairways, dramatic elevation changes, and challenging greens, the Pacific Nine quickly became a jewel of the Vancouver Island Golf Trail. The longer Highland Nine, which opened in 2010, brings the total course length to 6,603 yards. The driving range at Highland Pacific features a two-tiered tee line of covered and heated stalls, long and short game practice areas, lights for evening practice, and real terrain targets.

At 221 yards, the eighth hole is a quality golf hole in every sense of the word. This par 3 can be a real challenge from any of its tee boxes: the back two or even the much shorter 147-yard tee. The elevated tee and prevailing ocean breezes make club selection a crucial decision. A two-club difference is the norm because of the 35-yard drop in elevation. You have the ability to bail out short or right, but there will be a great deal of pride if you are even close to the pin on this gem. It's rated as the third-most difficult hole at Highland Pacific.

Photograph by Jeffrey Bosdet

NICKLAUS NORTH
Golf Course

PAR 3 ◆ 225 YARDS

Whistler, BC
800.386.9898
www.nicklausnorth.com

The legendary Jack Nicklaus created one of his finest courses in the shadows of Whistler and Blackcomb Mountains with his architectural skills on full display at the collection of great par-3 holes at Nicklaus North Golf Course. The 12th hole is a picturesque and prime example.

From the back tee box, the green is perched like an island 225 yards away at the far side of the deep blue pond. The green is well-bunkered, protected by a large sand trap front right between the water and the putting surface; another large bunker on the left side with two smaller ones to the back left; and a massive bunker back right that is shared with the third hole green complex. A classic Nicklaus design, the 12th requires the Golden Bear's signature high left-to-right iron shot.

The beauty and challenge of the 12th are consistent through the five tee boxes that range from the gold tee's 225 yards to the red tee's 102 yards. After hitting anything from long irons, hybrids, or mid-irons to wedges into the tiered green, you cross the pond on the beautiful stone Augusta-style bridge created in homage to the Hogan Bridge at Augusta National. If you make par, you'll feel that you've mastered the 12th.

Photograph by Rich Glass

NICKLAUS NORTH
Golf Course

PAR 3 ◆ 226 YARDS

Whistler, BC
800.386.9898
www.nicklausnorth.com

The dramatic 17th hole is the climax of five superb par-3 holes at Nicklaus North Golf Course. Unquestionably one of the most striking and challenging par 3s anywhere in golf, the hole traces the turquoise waters of glacier-fed Green Lake, the shoreline buttressed by massive river rocks. With the lake shimmering in front of the green complex, and all along the left side, the view from all of the five tee boxes is spectacular.

It is a thrilling shot from every tee: 226 yards, 213 yards, 188 yards, 163 yards, and 135 yards. From the tips in his 1998 Shell's Wonderful World of Golf match with Ernie Els, Fred Couples hit a five-iron to five feet for a remarkable birdie. The long bunker on the left side curls from the front all the way to the back of the green. There is another bunker on the right side, almost as

a reminder that there is plenty of room on the right for a safe, prudent shot. From there, it's a straightforward pitch shot to salvage par.

Before any thoughts of par, or even a birdie, the stunning view from the tee commands full attention. The lake, boulders, silica sand, and vibrant hues of the green are framed by two towering peaks in the distance—Wedge and Armchair Mountains—and Blackcomb on the right. Nicklaus saved the best of his par 3s for last.

Photograph by John Henebry

SALMON ARM
Golf Club

5^{HOLE}

PAR 3 ◆ 163 YARDS

Salmon Arm, BC
250.832.3667
www.salmonarmgolf.com

Tests on a golf course come in many forms. At 163 yards, the fifth hole at Salmon Arm Golf Club would seem to be a fairly routine short tee shot. With a dancing fountain in the blue-green waters of the pond and towering trees all around, its tranquil nature elicits a "take a big breath and enjoy the view" response.

This ideal little par 3 requires you to carry your tee shot over the pond onto the green. Shots hitting just short of the green will stop and roll back into the hazard; shots struck too firmly will bound through the green into a beautiful backdrop of fir, spruce, birch, and cedar trees.

The fifth green is friendly to shots out to the left or right, but you'll need to be on the correct side of the ridge to have a chance at a one-putt. The undulating three-level green is bisected left to right by a ridge, and balls coming to rest on the wrong side of the ridge will lead to a uniquely challenging putting experience.

Enjoy the view, but don't take it too easy as this hole has many small teeth that can bite you.

Photograph © hux.net

121

SANDPIPER

Golf Resort

Canadian course designer Russ Olson used the apparent simplicity of clear sightlines on Sandpiper Golf Resort's 177-yard 16th hole to create an intense mental challenge. From the tee, players can clearly see the green. There are no bunkers, so what's the problem? Well, clearly in the golfer's field of vision—inescapable, in fact—is a water hazard running almost the entire length of the fairway and green on the left side. The size of this body of water is nothing less than intimidating.

On the right side of this medium-length par 3, you're faced with the Harrison River, where wind gusts will capture the occasional tee shot. Also be sure to factor in the green, which measures only 19 yards wide and 37 yards deep. A miss left and you have found the water; a miss right and you'll find yourself with a difficult chip up to the green with the water hazard waiting just on the other side. Watch the wind direction, club well for the elevated green, and go for it. Birdies are a possibility.

All things considered, number 16 is a beauty of a hole. It is a treat to look at and a thrill to play.

Photograph by Doug Johnson

TALKING ROCK
Golf Course & Quaaout Lodge

15 HOLE

PAR 3 ◆ 210 YARDS

Chase, BC
800.663.4303
www.quaaoutlodge.com

You're privy to some of the best views of picturesque Little Shuswap Lake at Talking Rock Golf Course & Quaaout Lodge. Just a short drive from Kamloops or the Kelowna International Airport, this is one of British Columbia's most scenic locations, midway between Calgary and Vancouver.

As much as any other hole on the course, the 15th exemplifies the way in which course architects Cooke and Carleton have made use of the natural lay of the land in their design. Precision is the key to success here. The elevated par 3 demands accuracy to avoid the three bunkers protecting the front of the green. Not within the field of vision from the much higher tee boxes, an inhospitable band of rough between the tee and the bunkers that front the green will make you pay for falling short, while the elevated green drops off abruptly and steeply from the rear edge. Extra length is sure to land you in trouble. A full two clubs less off the tee is the best approach. And be aware, the green is separated into two sections sloping from the front to a much lower back right corner.

This hole is a great spot to showcase finesse and control.

Photograph © hux.net

WILDSTONE
Golf Course

6 HOLE

PAR 3 ◆ 152 YARDS

Cranbrook, BC
250.489.1282
www.WildstoneGolf.com

The Canadian Rockies are a global icon, and in the Kootenay Rockies region of British Columbia is one of the most majestic peaks, the highest in the area: Mount Fisher. As it commands all golfers' views, most dramatically from the practice range and then from the 18th hole, it is fitting that Fisher Peak is the inspiration for the Wildstone Golf Course logo.

At times, the views are overwhelming. The first Black Knight Design by Gary Player Design in Canada is so well routed along the scenic highlands above the city of Cranbrook that, despite its Rocky Mountain setting, walking is a welcome option.

The sixth hole, one of five par 3s, plays shorter than the distance on the scorecard as Wildstone is 3,000 feet above sea level.

There are eight possible tee boxes gradually lengthening the hole from 91 yards to 152 yards. For most players, the small pond in front of the tee is merely a scenic distraction, as is the glimpse of Fisher on the horizon and the saw-toothed edges of The Steeples range in the distance. The large receptive green is slightly elevated and open at the front but protected by a deep bunker on the left. Like the other 17 holes at Wildstone, the sixth is as photogenic as it is playable.

Photograph © hux.net

127

Redwood Meadows Golf & Country Club, page 143

Wolf Creek Golf Resort, page 165

ALBERTA

Desert Blume Golf Club, page 151

ALBERTA GOLF ASSOCIATION

Alberta, known as Wild Rose Country, is famous for its embodiment of the Canadian West, the Calgary Stampede, and the timeless beauty of the Rocky Mountains. And for the past century, from the Peace Country region to the US border, from the Foothills to the Great Plains, Alberta has earned an international reputation for spectacular golf courses.

The Alberta Golf Association was formed way back in 1908. Records show that during that first year, the AGA staged long drive competitions. Remarkably, given the equipment of the day, Mr. G. Shaw won the men's division with a prodigious clout that travelled a full 270 yards. Miss Mathieson captured the women's prize with a very respectable drive of 160 yards. Great tee shots have been flying around the province ever since.

When the AGA, now known as Alberta Golf, was incorporated as a society in 1912 to better serve its member clubs and help grow the fledgling game, there were just five clubs in the organization: the Lethbridge Country Club, Fort Macleod Golf Club, Calgary Golf and Country Club, Calgary's St. Andrews Golf Club, and the Edmonton Country Club. Today there are more than 250 member clubs with more than 60,000 individual members.

The game and the number of superb golf courses have also grown in every corner of Alberta over the past 100 years. And with outstanding events like the LPGA Tour's CN Canadian Women's Open, Canadian Tour events, and Skins Games, golf in Wild Rose Country just keeps getting better, as the spectacular courses included in this volume dramatically illustrate.

Photographs by Alberta Golf File Photography

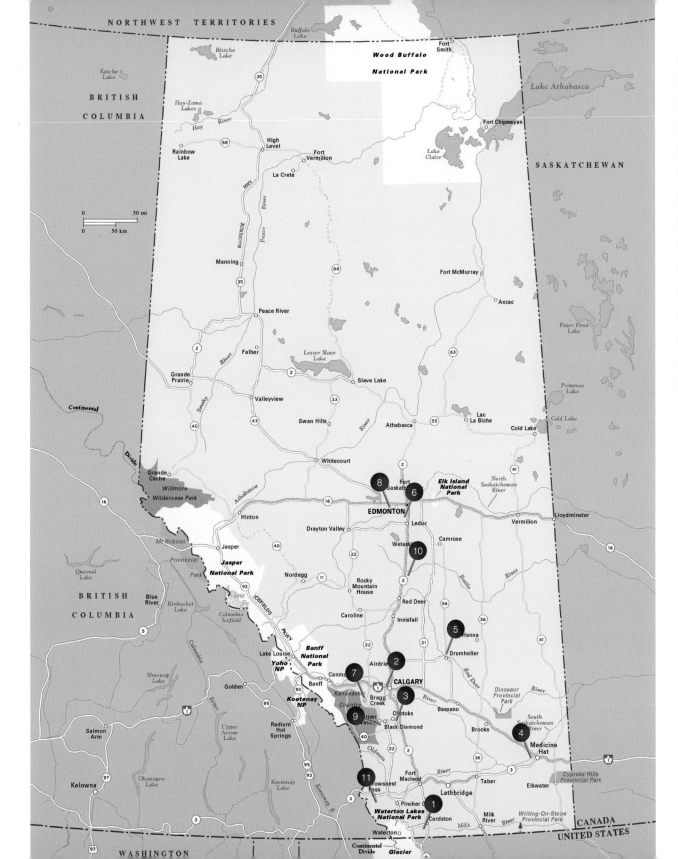

2 Canyon Meadows Golf & Country Club

3 Cottonwood Golf and Country Club

11 Crowsnest Pass Golf and Country Club

4 Desert Blume Golf Club

5 Dinosaur Trail Golf & Country Club

6 Edmonton Petroleum Golf and Country Club

1 Lee Creek Valley Golf Course

2 Lynx Ridge Golf Club

7 Redwood Meadows Golf & Country Club

2 Springbank Links Golf Club

2 The Glencoe Golf & Country Club

8 The Ranch Golf and Country Club

9 Turner Valley Golf Club

2 Valley Ridge Golf Club

10 Wolf Creek Golf Resort

CANYON MEADOWS

Golf & Country Club

18 HOLE

PAR 5 ◆ 585 YARDS

Calgary, AB
403.281.1188
www.canyonmeadowsgolf.com

The final hole at this private club, founded in 1957, forces players to keep their heads in the game as they approach the clubhouse for the potential rewards and settlement of friendly wagers.

A long sweeping dogleg, number 18 presents particular challenges. The elevation is tricky, as the fairway starts off level from the tee then slopes downhill to the green. What's more, hazards are in play for the entire hole. All along the right side, trees and rough will punish errant shots while a long fairway bunker defines the left corner of the dogleg.

A generous landing area off the tee might make it tempting to go for the green in two—especially after a perfect first shot—but be careful. Water guards the full left side of the green on the second shot as well as the width of the green's front, with bunkers to the front left and rear right. Players frequently display a tendency to go long on the third shot, but this makes for a difficult chip to a downhill sloping green.

Combining length with technical challenge, the final hole presents players with a good test to close the round. Play it well and go to the clubhouse with a well-earned sense of satisfaction. The alternative: a vivid reminder of just how demanding Canyon Meadows Golf & Country Club can be.

Photograph by John Sharpe

DESERT BLUME
Golf Club

PAR 5 ◆ 580 YARDS

Medicine Hat, AB
403.581.GOLF(4653)
www.desertblume.com

Desert Blume Golf Club's first hole is whimsically named "The Forest" for the solitary tree that stands in contrast to the surrounding cacti, sagebrush, and native grasses in the coulée formed by Seven Persons Creek. The remarkable natural site is the ideal setting for the Gary Browning-designed course.

The third hole brings all of the desert and links-style elements into play. The creek meanders the valley floor and flows across fairways and in front of greens 10 times, twice on the third hole alone. Named "Spotted Leopard Frog" for the species that is threatened elsewhere yet thrives here, the hole is a slight dogleg right and a true three-shot par 5 with the prevailing wind blowing into the players. The first shot from three of the four tee boxes must carry the creek, crossing the fairway about 100 yards from the back tees. The creek then traces the left side of the hole before cutting back across the fairway about 180 yards from the 20-yard-wide front to the green.

The massive putting surface is a full 41 yards deep, has three tiers, and is well-guarded with bunkers on the right, left, and front. The number one handicap hole is a beautiful and challenging welcome to Desert Blume.

Photograph by Plum Studios, Calgary, AB

THE GLENCOE
Golf & Country Club

7 HOLE

PAR 5 ◆ 566 YARDS

Calgary, AB
403.242.4019
www.glencoegolf.org

The Glencoe Golf & Country Club is truly a golfer's dream come true—a world-class course that is as beautiful as it is challenging. Designed and built under the exacting hand of master architect Robert Trent Jones Jr., these 45 holes on four unique layouts cover more than 440 acres.

The seventh hole of The Slopes course nestles into the sprawling meadows and offers scenic views of two of Glencoe's five nines and of the dramatic 25,000-square-foot clubhouse. With the spectacular Rocky Mountains as a backdrop, this 566-yard hole will challenge you regardless of your skill level. To be successful, strategically drive the ball to the first landing area that is well guarded with large spruce trees to the left and native grasses and penal bunkers to the right. The long hitter can go for the green in two; however, an additional large bunker to the right and a lake to the left leave little room for error.

Approach shots are hit into a green that is set above the water and heavily guarded by bunkers front left, back, and right. The green itself is undulating and sure to test your short game as well as your putter.

Photograph by J2Marketing

LYNX RIDGE
Golf Club

PAR 5 ◆ 550 YARDS

Calgary, AB
403.547.5969
www.lynxridge.com

Great par 5s are always defined by the options they present. Multiple hazards, long distances, intimidating turns, and unpredictable winds are just a few challenges that enhance the play. These are what keep experienced players challenged and what help newcomers to the sport improve.

At 550 yards, the sixth hole at Lynx Ridge Golf Club is certainly one of these par 5s. Its length makes it reachable for the longest of hitters and playable for those who focus less on distance and more on accuracy. A saddle-shaped, sloping fairway—a test in and of itself—greets you as you line up your tee shot. Well-struck tee shots will reach the crest of the hill and beyond, presenting a multitude of favourable, playable routes to get to the hole.

The longest hitters can try for the green in two if they dare—and only if they are confident in their ability to hit the target. Those laying up will need to avoid the ponds on each side of the fairway to stay out of trouble, which is certainly doable if accuracy is carefully attended to. The green itself is elevated and often calls for at least one extra club, regardless of skill level.

This is a true risk/reward par 5, which invites you to let loose and let a tee shot fly if you're willing to gamble on your talent. There is, however, enough length and enough trouble to make par difficult, if not impossible, from off the fairway, so choose your shots wisely and be prepared to accept the consequences.

Photographs: above by Wild Bob Productions; facing page by Bill Marsh

REDWOOD MEADOWS

Golf & Country Club

PAR 5 ◆ 556 YARDS

Redwood Meadows, AB
403.949.3663
www.redwoodmeadows.com

The setting is so natural and the surroundings so spectacular that while walking the lush fairways it is difficult to remember that Redwood Meadows Golf & Country Club is just a 20-minute drive from the bustling urban center of Calgary. Along the banks of the Elbow River, on the edge of the Foothills with views of the towering Alberta Rockies, the Tsuu T'ina Nation owns and operates one of the most beautiful and challenging courses in the country.

Renowned architect Bill Newis and Canadian golf legend Stan Leonard masterfully blended the 7,238-yard layout into the pristine terrain, opening the front nine in 1976 and the back in 1978. Tracing the river and the undulations of the meadowlands through the stands of poplar and spruce trees, Redwood is as memorable as it is playable.

Crystal-clear Rocky Mountain water is in play on seven holes and never more dramatically than on the 14th. A slight dogleg left and a true three-shot par 5, the hole has seven slightly elevated tee boxes and plays from 442 yards all the way back to 556 yards. With the Elbow River flowing along the entire right side of the hole, and a large pond pinching the landing area on the left, a tee shot in the fairway between the water hazards is ideal. The layup second shot must stay right of the creek and ponds along the left side, leaving a short iron into a small green that is well-protected by a rock-edged pond in front of the green. Scenic and strategic, the 14th is a classic par 5.

Photograph courtesy of Redwood Meadows Golf & Country Club

TURNER VALLEY
Golf Club

PAR 5 ◆ 555 YARDS

Turner Valley, AB
403.933.4721
www.turnervalleygolf.com

A great finishing hole, Turner Valley Golf Club's par-5 dogleg right can play long when the prevailing northwesterly winds are blowing down off the foothills of the Rocky Mountains. But if you have the ability to shortcut the fairway over the trees, the hole can become a birdie, or even an eagle opportunity.

The green is heavily protected with a large sand bunker running down the right side of the fairway from 75 yards out and all along to the green. The left side is also protected by two green-side bunkers, while the front of the green slopes to the left, causing many long approach shots to roll across into the waiting bunker. Locals call a front left pin placement a "sucker pin," for obvious reasons. Still, the right combination of nerves and shot-shaping will allow you to have bragging rights at the clubhouse. The hole has certainly inspired many a friendly wager over the years.

Demanding good length as well as accuracy, the hole frequently gives players additional pressure in making the final putt because of the viewing deck beyond. Still standing from the original 1928 schoolhouse, the building is now the clubhouse and deck, where a gallery of patrons and tournament participants can make golfers feel that they are putting for reputation or consolation.

Photograph by Gary Taylor

VALLEY RIDGE
Golf Club

PAR 5 ◆ 527 YARDS

Calgary, AB
403.221.9682
877.678.5188
www.valleyridgegolf.com

The meanderings of the Bow River through the ages have carved out a tranquil and idyllic setting for a golf course on the western edge of the bustling city of Calgary. Golfers could not be happier with the transformation of the former Happy Valley Recreation Area into Valley Ridge Golf Club. The well-designed property takes full advantage of the scenic natural landscape and offers a challenging variety of holes on the aptly named Valley and Ridge nines. The commanding presence of the Bow River and the skillful design of the layout are on full display on the eighth hole.

The Bow traces the entire left side of the tree-lined eighth, which plays 527 yards from the back tees. Requiring a strategic approach from all four tee boxes, the drive must carry a pond to reach the fairway, a full 240 yards from the blue tee. Trees on both sides narrow the landing area and a small bunker gathers errant shots to the right.

From the fairway, you're faced with a classic risk/reward decision: whether or not to challenge the pond and rock wall guarding the front of the green with the second shot. Shots too far right are blocked by trees, and the river is a constant companion on the other side. A large bunker protects the left side and a pot bunker guards the front right of the green that is 40 yards deep and slopes steadily from back to front. While a birdie on this beautiful hole is certainly possible if you challenge the green in two, golfers are happy with a par.

Photograph by Plum Studios, Calgary, AB

CROWSNEST PASS
Golf and Country Club

13 HOLE

PAR 4 ◆ 384 YARDS

Blairmore, AB
403.562.2776
www.crowsnestpassgolf.com

It is no overstatement to regard this course as the hidden gem of Alberta, a showcase of undulating terrain and strategic shot-making. A lot of golfers, even those who have played courses across the province, still haven't discovered the Crowsnest Pass Golf and Country Club, which has been ranked a one of the greatest values for your dollar. One thing is certain: play the course once, and you'll want to come back again.

A few of the holes are visible from the highway as it winds through the southernmost route from Alberta to British Columbia on the eastern edge of the Canadian Rockies. These windswept holes, with breathtaking views in every direction, are just a tease, giving the viewer no real idea of the rest of the course's stunning elevation changes. This is mountain golf at its finest.

Number 13 is a typical hole for the course. Definitely strategic, it starts with a tee shot that requires laying up short of the gorge that crosses the fairway and breaks it into

two segments. Long hitters may find resisting the temptation to go for it difficult, but in this situation, discretion is the better part of valour. Targeting the shot to the right of a tall fir tree, a lone sentinel set in the centre of the fairway, will give you the best opportunity of hitting the green in regulation.

Of course, anyone familiar with the area can tell you that the notorious Crowsnest Pass winds play an active role in every round. With a huge impact on length, the wind factors into club selection on almost every shot. A challenging course in an incredible setting, Crowsnest Pass is waiting to be discovered.

Photograph courtesy of Crowsnest Pass Golf and Country Club

DESERT BLUME
Golf Club

PAR 4 ◆ 420 YARDS

Medicine Hat, AB
403.581.GOLF(4653)
www.desertblume.com

The Desert Blume Golf Club course climbs down into the Seven Persons Creek coulée and rises back out of the valley with holes playing up and downhill. A fine example is the 16th hole, with tee boxes that are more than 50 feet above the creek, a pond, and a rock wall that must be carried to reach the fairway. After the exhilarating first shot on this par 4 that measures from 228 yards up to a robust 420 yards, it's all uphill.

The fairway doglegs slightly left, but the creek runs the length of the hole on that side and 100 feet below the fairway. That is why the hole is aptly known as "Cliff Hanger." The angle of the tee shot is based on bravery. A tee shot to the left side will shorten the approach, while one to the right is the safest option. A large fairway bunker on the right will catch any shot that is played too safely. Playing into the prevailing wind, and uphill, shots into the green require at least an extra club.

Two tiers wait on the 39-yard-deep putting surface. The bunker on the right is in the mid-back area of the green and ready to catch the shots of those who took too much extra club. The thrilling Cliff Hanger is the fourth handicap hole helping the 6,879-yard layout earn its 142 slope and 73.7 rating.

Photograph by Plum Studios, Calgary, AB

DINOSAUR TRAIL
Golf & Country Club

17 HOLE

PAR 4 ◆ 383 YARDS

Drumheller, AB
403.823.5622
www.dinosaurtrailgolf.com

You won't find a course with deeper historical connections than Dinosaur Trail Golf & Country Club. In the heart of the Alberta Badlands, the course site includes 75 million-year-old dinosaur bone beds. In fact, construction included consultation with a paleontologist to ensure no damage was done to this priceless natural heritage.

Dinosaur Trail actually plays like two courses. The older front nine stands out against the arid backdrop with its lush trees and expansive lake. The newer back nine makes full use of the area's natural assets: hoodoos and cacti follow the rugged rise and fall of the terrain, with fairways often broken into sections of green surrounded by rough. Stray off line, and the course can be unforgiving.

The par-4 17th presents particular challenges. Although relatively flat, it's demanding off the tee: your drive has to have a lot of carry if you're going to put yourself in scoring position. Accuracy is critical.

As with almost every hole on the back nine, the second shot requires focus and correct execution as the hole takes a sharp bend just left of the green. More players than naught play it wide to the right and approach the green in relative safety away from the hazard on the left. Yet players who take their shot across the coulée that guards the fairway's left side can expect a great opportunity for a birdie putt. Beware, though; the green is not large, and a grass bunker separates the green from the coulée on the front edge.

Photographs by Scott Westman

EDMONTON PETROLEUM

Golf and Country Club

PAR 4 ◆ 389 YARDS

Spruce Grove, AB
780.470.0700
www.epgcc.ab.ca

Former PGA Tour professional Mark McCumber and Mike Beebe & Associates have sculpted a masterpiece with the private Edmonton Petroleum Golf and Country Club, a 6,967-yard, par-72 championship course that truly captures the scenic nature of Northern Alberta and illustrates impeccable conditions.

The 11th's relatively short length may appear to be a relief, but it is a true test of skill. From the tee, the golfer is presented with a fairway that hugs the lateral water along the entire right side; an errant shot left and the ball will surely find the bunkers or fescue of this gradual dogleg right. A driver may be an option, but a fairway wood or hybrid should ensure your ball lands on the short grass.

When the wind is blowing, which is often the case, you must be especially cautious. A south wind allows a long hitter to get near or on the green, but the water extends threateningly all the way to the green's edge.

The approach shot from the fairway will be short with little room for error on the angled, narrow green. Hit long and you'll find yourself facing a difficult downhill bunker shot with water as a backstop. Hit too short and you'll be digging your ball out of the water.

On the quick, bentgrass green, everything slopes toward the water. Ideally you need to have an uphill putt, as speed control will provide an opportunity for birdie. Here, though, par will still allow you to leave with head held high.

Photograph by Michael Birdsell

LYNX RIDGE
Golf Club

HOLE 3

PAR 4 ◆ 420 YARDS

Calgary, AB
403.547.5969
www.lynxridge.com

Designed by golf and landscape architect Bill Newis—whose designs have been ranked in the top 50 courses in Canada—Lynx Ridge Golf Club serves up a broad spectrum of experiences on every round, just as the course has since its founding in 2000. Dramatic contours, strategically placed hazards, and a great variety of challenging holes are certain to deliver the joy of the game while challenging players of all abilities, which is one reason the club has developed such an impressive reputation.

Perched high above the banks of the beautiful Bow River—which affords golfers unbelievable views—the third hole at Lynx Ridge stands out as possibly the toughest on the course. It certainly has been known to break a few hearts when all is said and done.

At 420 yards, the hole requires a straight mid-length tee shot to reach the fairway and set up for the approach into the multitier green. Drives that sail left or right will be out of bounds or encounter hazards, requiring much skill and adding to the score to get back on target. Those that stray long will drop down into the gaping canyon that separates the fairway and the green; certainly something to avoid.

Once on the green, dramatic swales and contours make distance control critical and one-putts a challenge. On the green in two makes par a very attainable score. Miss the green, and even bogey becomes a challenge. You'll want to give your best on every shot on hole 3.

Photographs by Sarah Wirachowsky

THE RANCH
Golf and Country Club

5 HOLE

PAR 4 ◆ 423 YARDS

Acheson, AB
780.470.4700
www.theranchgolf.com

Designed by well-known golf and landscape architect Bill Robinson and located a few minutes west of Edmonton, The Ranch Golf and Country Club earned a place on *SCOREGolf* magazine's list of the province's top 15 public courses in 2011. From the scorecard, you might be fooled by the short, 6,500-yard distance from the back tees, but with a course rating of 141 this is certainly not a driver and seven-iron course.

The signature hole 5, a par 4, typifies the potential dangers that are apparent throughout the design. The back tees play to 423 yards and you're faced with a rolling fairway that slopes from left to right, making it imperative to hit the ball up the left side to avoid the deep rough and trees that line the red staked hazard on the right. If you hit right, be prepared to take your lumps

and chip back onto the fairway due to the overhanging trees that completely block out the view and line to the green. If you navigate your tee shot into the fairway, the second shot is no easy task. Any approach short of the green will be swallowed up by an enormous pit measuring 80 yards across and 60 yards deep. With three bunkers that surround a two-tiered green, which slopes heavily from back to front, a precise approach is a must if you want par. A three-putt is not out of the question on this quick undulating green.

Photograph by Agnieszka Clarke

THE RANCH 18
Golf and Country Club

HOLE

PAR 4 ◆ 439/350 YD

Acheson, AB
780.470.4700
www.theranchgolf.com

A dogleg right, The Ranch Golf and Country Club's hole 18, which measures 439 yards from the back tees, is one of the toughest tests of golf in Alberta. From the tee, you look out to a narrow fairway with water along the right side and laterally, on the left, coniferous and deciduous trees running the length of the fairway.

If your tee shot wasn't intimidating enough, the approach must carry more than 170 yards over water while avoiding a series of bunkers that protect the back to front sloping green. You might be inclined to play this unique hole from an alternative set of tees, as the fairway is split along the right of the water.

From the alternative back tees it measures 350 yards, so if you're a long hitter feel free to pull out the driver in hopes of a possible birdie, but be careful as the landing area is small and a creek protects the green. The smart play here is to lay up to 100 yards, wedge in below the hole, and then trust your putting. A shot above the hole can easily become a three-putt.

Photograph by Agnieszka Clarke

TURNER VALLEY
Golf Club

15 HOLE

PAR 4 ◆ 374 YARDS

Turner Valley, AB
403.933.4721
www.turnervalleygolf.com

The par-4 15th was given a new design in 2008, during Turner Valley Golf Club's course renovations, and now incorporates beautiful scenery and a historic setting. The hole has been designed to make the most of the natural terrain and for golfers to have a vantage point from which to pause for a moment and take in the stunning scenery. The surrounding sprawling cattle ranches and rolling foothills provide good opportunities for wildlife sightings. The fact that the property is home to cougars, moose, deer, coyotes, and many native bird species points directly to the course's ongoing commitment to its Audubon Sanctuary Program.

Made challenging by the pond that runs up the left side of the fairway and in front of the green, the fairway narrows from 35 yards at 235 yards off the tee, to 10 yards as you approach the green. A safe play is to lay up to 120 yards out for a second shot to a wide but shallow undulating green. But be careful, as water in front of the green can prompt a relaxed shot for a birdie or par to turn into bogey or worse. A shot hit too long will find the golfer having to play a delicate third shot from the native grasses to a downward sloping green, with water waiting for any ball that is hit with little spin. Cautious players often choose the bailout area to the green's right that leaves an easy pitch to the long part of the green. An opportunity for birdie is realistic, but whatever the score, the hole will be remembered for the beauty it has to offer.

Photograph by Gary Taylor

WOLF CREEK
Golf Resort

18 HOLE

PAR 4 ♦ 450 YARDS

Ponoka, AB
866.783.6050
www.wolfcreekgolf.com

Waving fescue, rolling hills, and distant horizons give the Wolf Creek Golf Resort an Old World feel. Architect Rod Whitman brings that links atmosphere to life on 36 holes of challenging and charming traditional golf. The 6,600-yard, par-70 Old Course opened in 1984, and the final nine of the 7,200-yard, par-71 Links Course opened in 2009, yet both layouts are so in tune with the landscape that they seem to have always been there.

The 18th hole on the Old Course—named "The Whit" in honour of the designer—is a superb example of Whitman's skill in creating classic links-style golf holes. From the four elevated tee boxes that stretch the par 4 from 365 to 450 yards, the pot bunker in the middle of the fairway serves as an aiming point on the slight dogleg right. Everything sweeps in that direction past the long

waste bunker, and pot bunkers guard the fairway where the terrain slopes and funnels balls into the middle.

When the wind blows from the northwest, the links design allows for a low, bump-and-run shot into the open front of the green; bunkers right and back, and a deep wheat grass bunker on the left, await errant attempts. The putting surface is long, slender, and gently rises into the mounding that frames the green complex. The 18th is a long, strong finishing hole reminiscent of the birthplace of golf.

Photograph by Chris Duthie

CANYON MEADOWS
Golf & Country Club

12 HOLE

PAR 3 ◆ 206 YARDS

Calgary, AB
403.281.1188
www.canyonmeadowsgolf.com

Making the most of the space afforded by a site of more than 200 acres backing onto Fish Creek Provincial Park, the classic parkland-style course of Canyon Meadows Golf & Country Club delivers an expansive layout and gives every hole a spacious, separate feeling.

Picturesque number 12 stands out as one of the toughest holes on the course. At a lengthy 206 yards, the signature par 3 makes use of significant hazards to create a visually intimidating prospect from the tee.

A sizable pond on the right side comes into play off the tee and runs the length of the fairway and the green. The water hazard is rock-lined as well, so steering well clear of it is the safe choice. The obvious solution is to play to the left. Not so fast! Players feel the need to bail out to the left away from the water, but to the left of the fairway and the green, two sizeable bunkers wait for shots that overcompensate.

The large green is relatively flat on the front approach, but slopes uphill at the midpoint and falls off to the right at the rear. Pin placement will dictate strategy on this hole, calling for both power off the tee and precise placement to make par. The 12th is certain to be a standout every round.

Photograph by John Sharpe

COTTONWOOD GOLF
and Country Club

12 HOLE

PAR 3 ◆ 195 YARDS

Dewinton, AB
403.938.7200
www.cottonwoodgcc.com

The private Cottonwood Golf and Country Club, nestled in the stunning Bow Valley a short drive from Calgary, is the inspiration of the Lyle Edwards family and once the site of Lawnie's Tree Farm. Many of the original plantings are still evident throughout the beautifully designed and maintained course.

Upon entrance to the property along the right side of the roadway, a majestic row of Swedish columnar aspens is your guide to the clubhouse, and on the left is your first view of the course's signature hole: the par-3 12th "island green."

From any of the five sets of tees, this hole is often described as breathtaking, especially with the ever-changing Alberta skies enhancing the beauty of the surrounding landscape as far as the eye can see.

If the magnificence of the hole is not enough to distract you, the prevailing winds from the south certainly might, so the focus should be on proper club selection with as much as a two- or three-club variance in attempt to hit the green. The hole is well bunkered, and errant shots require finesse to reach the green and have any opportunity for par.

Ranked as one of Calgary's most attractive and walkable courses and host to national and regional championships, the 6,900-yard course gives everyone a new perspective to the challenges and splendor of the game as well as lasting memories for those players fortunate enough to play the "Wood."

Photograph by Mark Skogen

LEE CREEK VALLEY
Golf Course

PAR 3 ◆ 189 YARDS

Cardston County, AB
403.653.4198
www.golfleecreek.com

Nestled in the picturesque foothills of the Canadian Rocky Mountains, Lee Creek Valley Golf Course—located just 14 miles north of the US border—is one of Alberta's most scenic and spectacular golf courses. Designed by celebrated architect Les Furber in 2005, the 6,782-yard layout traces the valley floor that gives the course its name, with Lee Creek and three ponds enhancing the setting. The 3,900-foot elevation provides incomparable mountain and valley views, and helps players carry their shots over the water, like the pond that defines the beautiful fourth hole.

One of four par 3s at the par-71 course, the fourth reflects the natural setting and plays from 90 yards all the way back to 189 yards. Like many of the tee boxes, the back tees are elevated with the foothills gently rising behind them. From these tees players look through a chute of stately cottonwoods and poplars over the pond to a green flanked by tall trees and smaller pines.

The putting surface is large—two club lengths deep—and undulating, the front sloping back toward the apron. There are no bunkers, and a berm running along the back of the green can act as a backstop for shots that carry too far. The raised area is well placed since the prevailing wind is from behind. Once past the hole's "wow" effect, golfers can focus on playing this excellent par 3.

Photograph courtesy of Lee Creek Valley Golf Course

LYNX RIDGE
Golf Club

PAR 3 ◆ 240 YARDS

Calgary, AB
403.547.5969
www.lynxridge.com

Ranging from 95 yards from the forward tees to 240 yards from the championship tees, number 14 at Lynx Ridge Golf Club is as long and demanding as it is beautiful.

Natural marshland separates the tees from the green and dense stands of mature poplar, aspen, and birch trees line the hole and grab errant tee shots.

Trying to reach this green on the first shot can be a challenge in itself, and careful club selection is as important as skill. A deep bunker lurks front and right for those who don't quite make the target. For those who are too aggressive and overshoot the green, a second trap lays in wait.

Once on the green, the distinct spine that dissects the putting surface makes one-putts very tricky, often giving even the most experienced players a run for their money. Golfers should focus on getting the ball on the same tier as the cup when they land on the green, or three- and four-putts are inevitable to complete the hole.

Every once in a while, a hole combines both scenery and challenge, making the experience simply perfect. The peaceful and tranquil setting at hole 14 lulls the golfer into a false sense of security, emitting the feeling of a lazy little hole that should be an easy par. Instead, the hole is every bit as difficult as any par 3, making a score of three or better a true accomplishment.

Photographs: above by Wild Bob Productions; facing page by Sarah Wirachowsky

THE RANCH

Golf and Country Club

14 HOLE

PAR 3 ◆ 177 YARDS

Acheson, AB
780.470.4700
www.theranchgolf.com

The Ranch Golf and Country Club was once the home of the Flying Red Wheel Ranch.

Situated on a site where the cowboys would look over grazing cattle, the beautiful downhill 177-yard hole 14 requires a great deal of accuracy, as it's guarded on the right by an extreme right-to-left sloping hillside covered in high fescue and trees.

A shot into this area and you'll have to rely on a delicate wedge shot to the green. Any ball hit a little strong will slowly begin to roll toward either the rocky creek that guards the left side of the undulating green or one of the bunkers that are so strategically placed to capture errant shots.

When the wind starts to blow, a bogey or worse can easily be expected on hole 14.

Photograph by Agnieszka Clarke

175

SPRINGBANK LINKS
Golf Club

5 HOLE

PAR 3 ◆ 165 YARDS

Calgary, AB
403.202.2000
www.springbanklinks.com

Hit this! From elevated tees overlooking the Bearspaw Reservoir, Springbank Links Golf Club's exciting par 3 truly represents the stunning topography and incredible vistas throughout the course.

Club selection is critical to carry the steep ravine that separates tee and green. It is truly one of those "time-stands-still" holes as your ball sails from the clubface, stalls in mid-flight, and then heads back down toward the green. Your group will be silent as the ball zeros in on the pin, listening for that sweet thud as your ball hits its target.

The green is inviting with a small back bowl, but there is trouble waiting in the aspen grove behind if you hit too long. A small bail-out area sits to the left, but if you are short, any attempt at par will require a high, crisp chip shot to recover.

Known for its reputation as one of Calgary's finer courses, Springbank has recently engaged the Ames Golf Group, directed by Stephen Ames, to further enhance an already exciting golf experience on this picturesque layout.

Hole 5 will definitely be part of your post-round recap as you share memories over a cool beverage or a fine merlot at one of the most beautiful and relaxing clubhouses in the province.

Photograph by Ava Heise

TURNER VALLEY
Golf Club

PAR 3 ◆ 168 YARDS

Turner Valley, AB
403.933.4721
www.turnervalleygolf.com

Turner Valley Golf Club is set in the shadow of the majestic Rocky Mountains and offers a unique experience for golfers. A blend of spectacular views, a great course, and echoes of the history of the hardworking men and women that built the modern province of Alberta are showcased here. In 1930, employees of Royalite Oil, the company responsible for development of the local area's oil reserves, created a sand green golf course that became the foundation for today's picturesque 6,800-yard, 18-hole layout: a course characterized by its tree-lined fairways and small, well-protected greens.

Looking down the hill from the par-3 10th hole, you can easily see the original mine that separated the towns of Turner Valley and Black Diamond. It's a spectacular setting for a hole that is deceptive in both length and ease of play. Elevation is the key here, with a 50-foot drop from tee to green. Adding to the complexity of this dramatic change in elevation are the ever-present winds.

The undulating green can be set up for many challenging pin placements that require accuracy and correct club selection. Depending on the winds that blow through the valley from the Rockies, your choice of clubs can vary up to three irons. A par can generally be a winner on this truly memorable hole.

Photograph by Gary Taylor

VALLEY RIDGE
Golf Club

17 HOLE

PAR 3 ◆ 245 YARDS

Calgary, AB
403.221.9682
877.678.5188
www.valleyridgegolf.com

From high on the ridge, the panoramic view to the Valley Ridge Golf Club 17th green and beyond is as spectacular as it is intimidating. The dramatic par-3 hole measures 245 yards from the blue tee box, and is only slightly less daunting from the 216-yard white, 195-yard yellow, and 177-yard red tees.

The tees tower 200 feet above the distant, well-protected green. All tee boxes require a precise and powerful shot through a chute formed by trees and then over a large stand closer to the green. The 17th usually plays with the prevailing wind, making careful club selection extremely important, as any shots long will be lost.

Two massive and deep bunkers define the left front and left back of the putting surface and a grass pot bunker guards the front. The trees lining the right side are on the edge of a creek, and the terrain slopes in that direction. Any shots long and right are in real trouble, while shots hitting the green have to be well placed. A large ridge running from the back of the green to the front creates two tiers and treacherous putts from the high side. Not surprisingly, the beautiful 17th yields the fewest holes-in-one of Valley Ridge's par 3s.

Photograph by Plum Studios, Calgary, AB

SPECTACULAR GOLF

WESTERN CANADA TEAM
ASSOCIATE PUBLISHER: Marc Zurba
SENIOR GRAPHIC DESIGNER: Emily A. Kattan
EDITOR: Michael Cunningham
CONTRIBUTING WRITER: Hal Quinn
PRODUCTION COORDINATOR: London Nielsen

HEADQUARTERS TEAM
PUBLISHER: Brian G. Carabet
PUBLISHER: John A. Shand
GRAPHIC DESIGNER: Lilian Oliveira
GRAPHIC DESIGNER: Paul Strength
MANAGING EDITOR: Rosalie Z. Wilson
EDITOR: Alicia Berger
EDITOR: Jennifer Nelson
EDITOR: Sarah Tangney
MANAGING PRODUCTION COORDINATOR: Kristy Randall
TRAFFIC SUPERVISOR: Drea Williams
ADMINISTRATIVE COORDINATOR: Amanda Mathers
CLIENT SUPPORT COORDINATOR: Kelly Traina
ADMINISTRATIVE ASSISTANT: Aubrey Grunewald

PANACHE PARTNERS, LLC
CORPORATE HEADQUARTERS
1424 Gables Court
Plano, TX 75075
469.246.6060
www.panache.com

Nicklaus North Golf Course, page 119

THE PANACHE COLLECTION

Dream Homes Series
An Exclusive Showcase of the
Finest Architects, Designers and Builders

Carolinas
Chicago
Coastal California
Colorado
Deserts
Florida
Georgia
Los Angeles
Metro New York
Michigan
Minnesota
New England

New Jersey
Northern California
Ohio & Pennsylvania
Pacific Northwest
Philadelphia
South Florida
Southwest
Tennessee
Texas
Washington, D.C.

Spectacular Homes Series
An Exclusive Showcase of the Finest Interior Designers

California
Carolinas
Chicago
Colorado
Florida
Georgia
Heartland
London
Michigan
Minnesota
New England

Metro New York
Ohio & Pennsylvania
Pacific Northwest
Philadelphia
South Florida
Southwest
Tennessee
Texas
Toronto
Washington, D.C.
Western Canada

Perspectives on Design Series
Design Philosophies Expressed
by Leading Professionals

California
Carolinas
Chicago
Colorado
Florida
Georgia
Great Lakes
London

Minnesota
New England
New York
Pacific Northwest
South Florida
Southwest
Western Canada

Art of Celebration Series
Inspiration and Ideas from
Top Event Professionals

Chicago & the Greater Midwest
Colorado
Georgia
New England
New York
Northern California
South Florida
Southern California
Southern Style
Southwest
Toronto
Washington, D.C.

City by Design Series
An Architectural Perspective

Atlanta
Charlotte
Chicago
Dallas
Denver
Orlando
Phoenix
San Francisco
Texas

Spectacular Wineries Series
A Captivating Tour of Established,
Estate and Boutique Wineries

California's Central Coast
Napa Valley
New York
Ontario
Sonoma County
Texas
Washington

Experience Series
The Most Interesting Attractions,
Hotels, Restaurants, and Shops

Austin & The Hill Country
Boston
British Columbia
Chicago
Southern California
Twin Cities

Interiors Series
Leading Designers Reveal Their Most Brilliant Spaces

Florida
Midwest
New York
Southeast
Washington, D.C.

Spectacular Golf Series
The Most Scenic and Challenging Golf Holes

Arizona
Colorado
Florida
Georgia
Ontario
Pacific Northwest
Texas
Western Canada

Weddings
Captivating Destinations and Exceptional Resources
Introduced by the Finest Event Planners

Southern California

Specialty Titles
The Finest in Unique Luxury Lifestyle Publications

21st Century Homes
Cloth and Culture: Couture Creations of Ruth E. Funk
Distinguished Inns of North America
Extraordinary Homes California
Geoffrey Bradfield Ex Arte
Napa Valley Iconic Wineries
Into the Earth: A Wine Cave Renaissance
Shades of Green Tennessee
Spectacular Hotels
Spectacular Restaurants of Texas
Visions of Design

Panache Books App
Inspiration at Your Fingertips

Download the Panache
Books app in the iTunes
Store to access select
Panache Partners
publications. Each book
offers inspiration at your
fingertips.

Panache Partners, LLC   1424 Gables Court   Plano, Texas 75075   469.246.6060   www.panache.com

INDEX